A. Y Hubbell

History of Methodism and the Methodist Churches of Staten Island

A. Y Hubbell

History of Methodism and the Methodist Churches of Staten Island

ISBN/EAN: 9783337162245

Printed in Europe, USA, Canada, Australia, Japan

Cover: Foto ©Lupo / pixelio.de

More available books at **www.hansebooks.com**

HISTORY OF

METHODISM

AND THE

METHODIST CHURCHES

STATEN ISLAND.

BY

A. Y. HUBBELL.

NEW YORK:

RICHMOND PUBLISHING COMPANY.

1898.

PREFACE.

We have endeavored in this book to collect and present to our readers the principal events in the history of Methodism on Staten Island. As far as possible we have gathered the information from the church records made at the time of the events narrated. When records have not been attainable great care has been exercised to get the most accurate data possible from those best able to give facts correctly.

As far as possible the work has been compiled by or under the immediate supervision of the pastors in charge of the different churches.

CONTENTS.

THE REV. HENRY BOEHM.

Born 1775.   Died at Woodrow 1875.   Seventy-four years
in the Ministry.

METHODIST EPISCOPAL CHURCHES

OF STATEN ISLAND.

CHAPTER I.

ORIGIN AND PROGRESS OF METHODISM IN ENGLAND.

THE REV. JOHN WESLEY, the founder of Methodism, was born 1703 O. S. In 1725 he was ordained a deacon of the Church of England. Three years later he took priestly orders. At this time he was his father's curate, but soon afterward left his curacy and returned to Oxford at the call of the rector of his college.

It was while at Oxford that the title of Methodists was first applied to Mr. Wesley and his associates, about fifteen in number. They were so conscientious and regular in their religious duties, observing fasts every Wednesday and Friday, visiting the sick and the poor, meeting for religious conversation and reading the scriptures, that a rude youth of Christ's church, observing the exact regularity of their lives and studies, characterized them in derision as a "new set of Methodists" in allusion to a class of ancient physicians who assumed that name.

But the principal characteristics which distinguish the Methodist Episcopal church came into Mr. Wesley's life a few years later.

In 1835 he came to America as a missionary to the colony of Georgia and the American Indians. On the voyage he fell in with a company of devout Moravians. On one occasion they experienced a storm, but the Moravians held their religious service as usual. During the singing of the Psalm, with which the service opened, the sea broke over the vessel, split the mainsail into pieces and poured in between the decks. A terrible screaming began among the English, but the Moravians continued their service as calmly as if nothing unusual or dangerous had happened. "I asked one of them afterward," writes Mr. Wesley, 'Were you not afraid?' He answered, 'I thank God, no.' I asked, 'But were not your women and children afraid?' He mildly replied, 'No; our women and children are not afraid to die.'" These things and his conversation with pious Moravians convinced Mr. Wesley that there was something more in religion than the belief in the creeds and submission to the laws of Christ and to the rules and services of the church acted out day by day and hour by hour, in all the prescribed means and services of the church, and in the general duties of life.

In 1738 Mr. Wesley returned home much dissatisfied with his spiritual condition. Of himself he writes at this time, " I went to America to convert the Indians, but O! who shall convert me? Who is he that will deliver me from this evil heart of unbelief?" But two months later in writing of his conversion he says, "I felt my heart strangely warmed. I felt I did trust in Christ, Christ alone, for my salvation. And an assurance was given me that he had taken away my sin, even mine, and saved me from the law of sin and death."

We see, therefore, that Mr. Wesley had been a priest of the English church for ten years, living a most conscientious and exemplary Christian life before his conversion.

His own experience, therefore, led him to adopt very different views of conversion and salvation from that held by the English church.

The new doctrine of the Wesleys, their associates and followers, which was a condemnation of the English church, drew down upon them the wrath of both the clergy and laity, and they were obliged to preach in the open air. This offended the clergy still more. Among the followers of Mr. Wesley were a number of clergymen of the church of England, and these and Mr. Wesley administered the priestly offices for their converts until their numbers became too great and the territory too large for the labors of so few laborers.

The following rules were adopted by these early Methodists for conducting their services and governing their religious life:

1. That they would meet together once a week, to confess their faults one to another, and pray one for another that they might be healed.

2. That the persons so meeting should be divided into several bands, or little companies, none of them consisting of fewer than five, or more than ten persons.

3. That every one, in order, should speak as freely, plainly, concisely as he could, the real state

of his heart, with his several temptations and deliverances since the last time of meeting.

4. That all the bands should have a conference every Wednesday evening, beginning and ending with singing and prayer.

5. That any who desire to be admitted to this society should be asked: What are your reasons for desiring this? Will you be entirely open, using no kind of reserve? Have you any objection to any of our orders?

6. That when any new member was proposed, every one present should speak clearly and freely of whatever objection he might have of him.

7. That those against whom no reasonable objection appeared should be, in order for their trial, formed into one or more district bands, and som? person agreed on to assist them.

8. That, after two months' trial, if no objection appeared, they should be admitted into the society.

9. That every fourth Saturday should be observed as a day of general intercession.

10. That on Sunday seven-night following, there should be a general love-feast, from seven till ten in the evening.

11. That no particular member should be allowed to act in anything contrary to any order of the society; and that if any persons, after being therein admonished, should not conform thereto, they should not longer be esteemed as members.

It will be seen from the above rules, how closely the Methodist Episcopal church has followed the plans first laid down by its distinguished founder.

It will be remembered that up to this time all the religious services were conducted by regularly ordained clergymen of the English church, but the number of clergymen who joined Wesley were so few and their followers so numerous that the movement seemed in danger of being greatly retarded by the lack of preachers. The majority of the English clergymen not only refused to let the Methodist ministers officiate in their churches, but also refused to administer the sacrament of the Holy Communion to their followers, and actually drove them from the altar.

We cannot give the next step in the progress of Methodism better than by quoting from Porter's "Compendium of Methodism:"

"Another necessity to be provided for, arising from the growing state of the societies, was the increasing demand for laborers. Mr. Wesley's desire was that the established clergy should watch over such as he and his associates had brought to repentance, and encourage them in faith and practice, as their spiritual interest required. But they did no such thing. They conducted toward them, in most cases, more like wolves than shepherds, ridiculing their religion, repelling them from the Lord's table, and otherwise hindering rather than helping them. The result was, many turned back to the world and plunged into sin, as their legal pastors taught them.

"How to remedy this difficulty was a question. Every society needed a pastor; but pastors were few, and these must travel all over the kingdom. This suggested the selection of some one from among themselves, of deep piety, and sound judgment in divine things, and request him to meet the others and confirm them, by reading, conversation and prayer as he might be able.

"No other plan seemed at all practicable, and this would not always serve well, for the want of the right style of men, as we have seen in the case of Mr. Cennick, who was one of the first appointed to this office, and the very first to divide the society and set up an independent meeting.

"The society in London had suffered much from false teaching, and been considerably scattered. Therefore, as Mr. Wesley was about to leave the city, he appointed a young man, a Mr. Maxfield, whom he considered sound in the faith, to meet at the usual times, and by such means as were suitable for a layman, to encourage the members to stand forth in the liberty wherewith Christ had made them free. Being fervent in spirit, and mighty in the scriptures, he pleased and profited the people greatly and demonstrated the wisdom of the lay pastorate involved in this novel scheme.

"But Providence had designs beyond the mere establishment of the little flock. The talent and energy of Maxfield attracted many to his meetings, whose attention indicated that they were a people prepared for the Lord. This led him a little further than he had designed, or than was consistent with the prevailing notions of the church order at that time.

"He began to preach. But notwithstanding it was not quite orderly, the Lord blessed the effort, and many were deeply awakened and brought to the joyful knowledge of the truth. This, however, did not justify the 'irregularity' in the esteem of some. There are individuals in most places who hold church order above every other consideration. God must work by their rules, and sinners be con-

verted in their way, or there will be trouble. So it
was in this case. While not a few rejoiced in the glorious results of this strange innovation, many
trembled for the honor of the priestly office, and
complaint was heard on all sides.

"Mr. Wesley, being directly informed of the disor-
der, hastened to London to arrest it. But before he
came to the immediate agent of the trouble, the
timely advice of his ever considerate and pious
mother moderated his displeasure, and suggested
the propriety of an examination, which at first was
not thought necessary. Seeing on his arrival that
something troubled him, she inquired what it was;
to which he abruptly replied, 'Thomas Maxfield has
turned preacher, I find.' Looking him attentively in
the face, 'John,' said she, 'you know what my senti-
ments have been. You cannot suspect me of favor-
ing readily anything of this kind. But take care
what you do with respect to that young man, for
he is as surely called of God to preach as you are.
Examine what have been the fruits of his preaching, and hear him for yourself.' He did so and was
constrained to say, 'It is the Lord. Let him do
what seemeth to him good.'

"'In other places, also,'' says the biographer of Mr.
Wesley, "'the same assistance was afforded. But
he submitted to it with reluctance. His high
church principles stood in his way. But such ef
fects were produced that he frequently found himself in the condition of Peter, who, being questioned
in a matter somewhat similar, could only relate the
fact, and say, 'What was I, that I could withstand
God?'

"But the Lord was about to show him greater

things than these. An honest man, a mason of
Bristol, in New Yorkshire, whose name was John
Nelson, coming up to London to work at his trade,
heard that word which he found to be the 'power
of God unto salvation.' Nelson had full business
in London, and large wages. But from the time of
making his peace with God it was continually on
his mind that he must return to his place and
work among his people. He did so about Christmas
in the year 1740. His relations and acquaintances
began to inquire what he thought of this new faith?
And whether he believed there was any such thing
as a man knowing that his sins were forgiven?
John told them point-blank, 'that this new
faith, as they called it, was the old faith of the gospel; and that he himself was as sure that his sins
were forgiven as he could be of the shining of the
sun.' This was soon noised abroad and more and
more came to inquire concerning these things.
Some put him upon proofs of the great truths which
such inquiries naturally led him to mention. And
thus he was brought unawares to quote, explain,
compare and enforce several parts of the scripture.
This he did at first, sitting in his house, till the
company increased so that the house could not
contain them. Then he stood at the door, which
he was commonly obliged to do in the evening when
be came from his work. God immediately set his
seal to what was spoken; and several believed and
therefore declared that God was merciful, also to
their unrighteousness, and had forgiven their sins.

"Here was a preacher and a large congregation,
many of whom were happy partakers of the faith of
the gospel, raised up without the direct interference

of Mr. Wesley. He therefore now fully acquiesced in the order of God, and rejoiced that the thoughts of God were not as his thoughts."

Thus we have the origin of lay preaching, to which Methodism, under God, is so much indebted.

From the same authority we give the origin of class meetings: " 'At length,' Mr. Wesley remarks, 'while we were thinking of quite another thing, we struck upon a method for which we have cause to bless God ever since. I was talking with several of the society in Bristol concerning the means of paying the debts there; when one stood up and said, 'Let every member of the society give a *penny* a week till all are paid.' Another answered, 'But many are poor and cannot afford to do it.' 'Then,' said he, 'put eleven of the poorest with me, and if they can give anything, well. I will call on them weekly, and if they can give nothing, I will give for them as well as for myself. And each of you can call on eleven of your neighbors weekly; receive what they give, and make up what is wanting.' It was done. In a while some of these informed me, 'they found such and such a one did not live as he ought.' It struck me immediately, 'this is the thing, the very thing we have wanted so long.' I called together all the leaders of the classes, (so they called the collectors) and desired that each would make a particular inquiry into the behavior of those whom he saw weekly. They did so. Many disorderly walkers were detected. Some turned from the evil of their ways. Some were put away from us. Many saw it with fear, and rejoiced unto God with reverence.'

"The same arrangement was soon adopted in condon, an l in all the other societies, with the happiest effect. Each leader was required to see every member of his class once a week, at least, to inquire after the prosperity of their souls; to advise, reprove, or exhort, as it was found necessary; to receive what they were disposed to give for the relief of the poor; and to meet the minister and stewards, etc., as at the present time. This arrangement, we believe, has never been abrogated i a y branch of the Methodist family, and it is to b: hoped that it never will be. But at first the leaders visited the members at their own houses. This was soon found to be very inconvenient, and in some cases impracticable. Hence it was agreed that the members of each class should meet together once a week, and the leader was required to visit only those who might be absent. So much for the history of our classes."

CHAPTER II.

THE ORIGIN AND ORGANIZATION OF THE METHODIST EPISCOPAL
CHURCH IN AMERICA.

BY THE REV. W. S. MC COWAN, D. D.

It will be of interest to our readers to give a short account of the origin and organization of the Methodist Episcopal church in America. In so doing we would express our indebtedness to such authorities as "Porter's Compendium of Methodism" and "Daniel's Illustrated History of Methodism" for facts furnished.

The first Methodist society in this country was organized in the city of New York, in the year 1766. It was composed of emigrants from Ireland who had been converted at home and joined the Wesleyons. Coming among strangers where vital piety was at a low ebb and sinful pleasure the idol of all classes of the community, they turned away from the simplicity of the cross and went into the follies and vanities of the world. But there was a "Mother in Israel" among them, who, feeling that their course demanded a rebuke, trusting in their respect for her age and in God for the success of the measure, she rushed into the room where they were assembled, seized the cards with which they were playing, and threw them into the fire. She now ex-

horted them to turn from their backsliding and to
Philip Embury, one of the party, but formerly a
preacher, she said: "And you must preach to us
or we shall all go to hell together and God will re-
quire our blood at your hands. ' When he objected
that he had neither house nor congregation, she
replied: "Preach in your own house first and to our
own company." He yielded to her earnest appeal
and preached the first Methodist sermon ever de
livered in this country, in his own hired house and
to a congregation of five persons.

In the year 1765, Capt. Webb, an officer in the
English army, was awakened and converted under
the ministry of Mr. Wesley. Being appointed to
service in the British army in America, on his
arrival in New York, hearing of the little society in
the city, he soon appeared in the midst of them in
his official costume and awakened no little interest.
Such was the success of Capt. Webb's preaching
that the room in which they were accustomed to
meet was filled to overflowing and the society was
obliged to seek other accommodations. A rigging-
loft in William street was hired, which, however, did
not answer the purpose long. The rapid increase
in numbers suggested the erection of a meeting
house, which, after much prayer, planning and beg-
ging, resulted in the building of the old John street
church. This was the first Methodist meeting-house
in America and was dedicated to the worship of
Almighty God, Oct. 30th, 1768, about thirty years
after the birth of Methodism in England.

Upon request being made to Mr. Wesley, two
missionaries, Richard Boardman and Joseph Pilmore,
were sent, who arrived in Philadelphia, Oct. 24th, 1769.

Mr. Boardman went to New York and commenced his labors in the city and the surrounding country. Mr. Pillmore with Robert Strawbridge, a local preacher from Ireland, ministered to the society in Philadelphia which had been formed by Capt. Webb, and extended the field of their labors into Maryland, Virginia and North Carolina. Other ministers were sent out to aid the growing work. In Oct. 1771, Messrs. Francis Asbury and Richard Wright arrived as missionaries sent out by Mr. Wesley. Mr. Asbury labored in New York and vicinity during the winter and extended his labors into all parts of the country. In the summer of 1773, two other missionaries arrived, Messrs. Thomas Rankin and George Shadford.

It may be of interest to note the appointments of the preachers made at the first conference in Philadelphia, presided over by Mr. Rankin. They were as follows: New York, Thomas Rankin; Philadelphia, George Shadford; New Jersey, John King and William Waters; Baltimore, Francis Asbury, Robert Strawbridge, Abraham Whitworth and Joseph Yearbry; Norfolk, Richard Wright; Petersburg, Robert Williams.

In spite of the difficulties originating in the American War of Independence, the Methodist societies continued to prosper and increase, so that in 1784 there were eighty-three traveling preachers and fourteen thousand nine hundred eighty-six members.

The necessities of the case, the growth of Methodism, now demanded its organization as a church, a ministry having authority to administer the sacraments. It was plain that something must be done or there would be a division in the body. Mr. Wesley had watched the progress of events, the demand for regularly ordained ministry, and was prepared for the crisis. In Sept. 1784, Mr. Wesley, according to the custom of the English church, assisted by the Revs. Thos. Coke and James Creighton, ordained Messrs. Whatcoat and Vasey as deacons, and on the following day as presbyters or elders. In addition to this he performed a separate act of consecration upon Dr. Coke as superintendent of the Methodist societies in America, which office Coke was to convey to Asbury, and Coke and Asbury were to be joint superintendents of all the brethren in America.

The following credential was given to Dr. Coke by Mr. Wesley:

"*To all to whom there present shall come, John Wesley, late Fellow of Lincoln College in Oxford, Presbyter of the Church of England, sendeth greeting.—Whereas many of the people in the southern provinces of North America, who desire to continue under my care and still adhere to the doctrine and discipline of the Church of England, are greatly distressed for want of ministers to administer the sacraments of Baptism and the Lord's Supper, according to the usage of the same church, and whereas there does not appear to be any other way of supplying them with ministers,*

"*Know all men that I, John Wesley, think myself to be providentially called at this time to set apart some persons for the work of the ministry in America, and therefore under the protection of Almighty God and with a single eye to His glory, I have, this day, set apart as a superintendent, by the imposition of my hands and prayer (being assisted by other ordained ministers) Thomas Coke, doctor of civil law, a presbyter of the Church of England and a man whom I judge to be well qualified for that great work. And I do hereby recommend him to all whom it may concern as a fit person to preside over the flock of Christ.*

" In testimony whereof, I have hereunto set my hand and seal, this second day of September, in the year of our Lord, one thousand seven hundred and eighty-four.

"John Wesley."

Mr. Wesley writes in his letter to the brethren in North America, dated Bristol, Sept. 10th, 1784: "Lord King's account of the primitive Church convinced me many years ago, that bishops and presbyters are the same order and consequently have the same right to ordain. And as the Methodist church was organized before either the Roman or the Anglican ordinations in this country, so it is the first regularly established Episcopal church in America.

The first American General Conference was held in the Lovely Lane Church, Baltimore, Dec. 24th, 1784. Sixty ministers were present. Bishop Coke presided, "and we agreed," writes Asbury, " to form ourselves into an Episcopal church and to have superintendents, elders and deacons." On the second day of the session Asbury was ordained deacon by Dr. Coke, assisted by Elders Whatcoat and Vasey. On the third day, which was Sunday, Asbury was ordained elder and on Monday he was consecrated as superintendent by Bishop Coke, his friend Otterbein of the German Reformed Church and the elders assisting in the solemn service. Several deacons and twelve elders were also ordained, rules of discipline adopted and the conference ended in great peace and unanimity. This is known as the "Christmas Conference."

Such was the origin and organization of the Methodist Episcopal Church in America. And as no essential change in its construction has since been made, it is unquestionably true, as stated by Bishop Simpson in his reply to Deacon Stanley, on the occasion of the reception of the latter in St. Paul's Methodist Episcopal Church, New York, that "there is no other organization or communion on earth, which so clearly and distinctly represents the mind of John Wesley as the Methodist Episcopal church."

WOODROW M. E. CHURCH,

WOODROW, S. I.

WOODROW M. E. CHURCH.
Woodrow.

CHAPTER III.

BY THE REV. M. S. LAMBERT.

WOODROW METHODIST EPISCOPAL CHURCH may well be called the mother of Methodism on Staten Island. Bethel, St. Mark's and St. John's are the direct offspring of Woodrow, while St. Paul's is the offspring of Bethel and the granddaughter of Woodrow.

This sort of parental spiritual relationship lends to Woodrow Church a peculiar and tender interest in the hearts of all the Methodists on Staten Island.

The history of this old church dates from one November night in 1771 when Francis Asbury, one of the great pioneers of Methodism in America, came across the old Blazing Star ferry, on his way from Philadelphia to New York, and landed at Rossville where there were not more than half a dozen houses.

He called the sparsely settled hardy farmers together at the residence of Peter Van Pelt, and expounded to them the principles of Methodism as he had learned it direct from the lips of its great founder, John Wesley.

This house, the cradle of Methodism, was an old Dutch house with low, sloping roof, wide fire-place and small windows, and stood on the shore road.

The site is now occupied by the Joshua Wright house and is near the present St. John's M. E. Church. Although the house which was the birthplace of Methodism on Staten Island has long since become dust and ashes, the spiritual movement started there has never wavered nor faltered. Methodism, which was then a strange, new doctrine, with not a single follower on the Island, and not more than eleven hundred in America, with ten unordained preachers to spread its glorious truths, now counts its ministers by the thousands and its converts by the hundred thousands.

This small beginning in the humble farm-house of plain old Peter Van Pelt has spread all over Staten Island, and sent thousands of dollars to carry the light of the gospel to foreign lands.

During the years that followed the introduction of Methodism on Staten Island, occasional services were held at different houses, and about this time Staten Island was placed in charge of the preachers stationed at Elizabethtown, N J. In their work they were greatly assisted by local preachers and class-leaders.

Among the earliest of these were William Cole and Joseph Totten. William Cole was licensed May 6th, 1792, ordained deacon Oct. 1st, 1797, and elder June 2nd, 1822. He died April 14th, 1843. aged 73 years. Joseph Totten was one of the first members of the Methodist society on Staten Island and was licensed to preach in 1792. He died in Philadelphia in 1818.

Among the first converts to and staunch advocates of Methodism in these early days, were the Dissosways, Tottens, Coles,   ..tes, Seguines, Wogloms, Winants, Drakes, Bedells, Van Pelts, Woods,

Guyons, Latourettes, Journeays, La Forges, Hilliers, and others whose descendants have remained stead-fast in the faith of their fathers, and who are still leading members of the denomination in Westfield.

The first record we have of the organization of a Methodist society is at a meeting held May 5th, 1787, at the house of Abraham Cole. The meeting was called for the purpose of taking steps toward build-ing a Methodist Episcopal church on Staten Island. Nine trustees were chosen: Abraham Cole, Benja-min Drake and John Hillier, first class, to serve one year; Gilbert Totten, John Sleight and Joseph Wood, second class, to serve two years; Joseph Totten, Elias Price and Israel Disosway, third class, to serve three years.

The meeting determined to raise money to build a place of worship and on the 7th of June a paper was drawn up and circulated for subscriptions toward the proposed church.

This call for money was responded to in a very liberal manner as will be seen from the list of sig-natures appended thereto, of which we give a copy :

To all charitable, well-disposed Christians of every denomination on Staten Island :

WHEREAS, The inhabitants on the west end of said Island are destitute of any place of public worship, so that numbers, more especially of the poorer and middling ranks of people, who have not carriages, etc , are necessarily precluded from attending the worship of God, their children also lose the benefit of public instruction, and it is to be feared the conse-quence will be to the rising generation a settled contempt for the worship of God, and the ordinances of His House.

To remedy as far as human prudence can extend, the afore-said and many other inconveniences that might be named, the members of the Methodist Episcopal church on said Island have chosen trustees agreeable to law, in order to erect a church for the performance of divine service, and 'tis supposed by the blessing of God, this may be the means of not only benefiting the present generation, but that numbers yet unborn may have reason to praise God for the pious care of their forefathers. But as this will be attended with a heavy expense, to which the members of said church are inadequate, they hereby respectfully solicit the donation of all such as are willing to promote so laudable an undertaking. We, therefore, the subscribers, do hereby promise to pay, or cause to be paid to the said trustees, or any person empowered by them to receive it, the sums affixed to our several names, as witness our hands this seventh day of June in the year of Our Lord one thousand seven hundred and eighty-seven.

	£.	s.	d.
Gilbert Totten	8	0	0
Israel Disosway	15	0	0
Benjamin Drake			
£8 if he keeps that land now in dispute; £4 if he loses it			
Andrew Prior	1	0	0
Nicholas La Forge	0	16	0
Charles La Forge	0	16	0
Sarah Albouy	0	4	0
Joseph Totten	8	0	0
Richard Dubois	2	10	0
James Eddy	1	4	0
Charles Stover	4	15	0
Thomas Totten	1	10	0
Samuel Skinner	1	0	0
Joseph Bedell	0	4	0
Abraham Rickhow	1	10	0
Mark Disosway	5	0	0
Catherine Androvette	1	0	0
Robert Donaly	0	8	0
Ashur Tappin	1	0	0
James Johnson, Sr	0	4	0
Leah Tappin	1	0	0
Peter Winant (blacksmith)	2	0	0
Peter Woglom	6	0	0
John Marshall	3	0	0
Mary Woglom	0	10	0
Catherine Woglom	0	8	0
John Winant, S M	0	8	0

	£.	s.	d.
Joshua Wright	5	0	0
John Woglom	2	0	0
Nathaniel Harriet	0	8	0
Belacha Butler	1	0	0
John Androvette	5	0	0
John Prior	1	0	0
Abraham Cole (boatman)	2	0	0
Ephraim Johnson	2	0	0
James Johnson (weaver)	1	0	0
William Eddy	1	0	0
Peter Woglom. Jr	0	8	0
Abraham Woglom, Jr	0	8	0
John Stouttenborough	1	0	0
Peter Winant	0	8	0
Jacob Slaght	0	8	0
Bornt Parlee	0	8	0
Richard Cole	0	4	0
John Slaght Sr	0	4	0
Benjamin Swain	0	8	0
Abraham Marshall	0	8	0
Abner Taylor	0	4	0
Benjamin Lizelere	1	2	0
Bornt Slaght	0	9	0
Nicholas Journeay	0	8	0
Benjamin Micheau	0	16	0
Benjamin Woglom	0	8	0
Christian Wright	0	10	0
William Thorn	0	8	0
Henry Slaght	0	12	0
Elizabeth Slaght	1	0	0

	£.	s.	d.		£.	s.	d.
Isaac Cole	0	4	0	Richard Taylor	0	16	0
John Slaught	4	15	0	Joseph Macdaniel	1	0	0
Henry Seguine	1	0	0	Widow Mary Winant	0	10	0
Henry Relay	1	10	0	Dower Johnson	0	8	0
Abraham Johnson	0	8	0	James Latourette	1	0	0
John Dubois	1	0	0	Hester Mersereau	0	4	0
Jacob Rickhow	5	0	0	R. Henderson	0	16	0
Mathew Bun	1	0	0	Charles Morgan	0	12	0
John Dubois, Sr	1	5	0	Polly Eddy	0	6	0
Abigal Praul	1	0	0	Lewis Praul	1	10	0
Thomas Butier	3	4	0	Isaac Praul	2	0	0
Henry Parlee	0	8	0	Peter Winant, Sr	4	15	0
Nancy Woglom	0	16	0	Abraham Johnson (weaver)	0	8	0
Jacob Seguine	0	4	0	Abraham Woglom	4	10	0
Widow Hester Hillier	0	4	0	Richard Conner, Jr	0	8	0

Here ends the original subscription list. Others doubtless contributed of whom no record is made.

There must have been hustlers on Staten Island in those days, for although the subscription paper was not drawn up until June 7th the church was dedicated the same year. "Many hands make light work" and "willing hearts make nimble fingers," and we can readily believe that those pious pioneers put their shoulders to the wheel and every one helped to forward the work and it was with no little pride that they saw their church opened for worship.

We have no record of these first dedication services, but it was undoubtedly a time of great rejoicing, and the farmers and their families came from all parts of the Island to witness so notable an event.

The first church edifice, constructed of wood, was somewhat smaller than the present one, though sufficiently large to meet all demands. It was built parallel with the road, its greater dimensions being from east to west. The principal entrance faced the highway, being practically on the side. There was also an entrance at the west end; but this was

only kept open during the milder seasons of the
year. From the west-side entrance a stairway on
either hand led to the gallery, which extended along
three sides of the building. The pulpit was in the
east end, and was constructed somewhat after the
pattern of a large urn. Above the pulpit was suspended a wooden canopy, surmounted by a small
cone, and serving the double purpose of sounding-
board and ornament. A flight of steps led into this
box-like affair, and here, removed from all intrusion,
the preachers of those days dispensed the Word of
Life. Light was admitted through double rows of
windows, arranged respectively above and below the
gallery.

There were no cushions in the old-fashioned,
open-backed benches, nor any carpet on the floor;
but as a substitute for the latter white sand was
resorted to, and even within the sacramental rail
this was considered a sufficient covering. The
communion table, harmonizing with the surroundings, was exceedingly plain, not made of mahogany,
walnut, or cherry, but of common pine. The
long benches on the north side of the preacher's
desk were reserved for the officiary and honored
fathers of the church, while those on the south side
were occupied by the more sedate and devout of
elect ladies. The congregation likewise, at least in
regard to sex, were similarly divided, so that men
sat on one side and women on the other. Stoves
were a luxury not enjoyed for years, and a goodly
number were accustomed to take their heated bricks
or foot-pans with them when they wended their way
to the sanctuary. The offerings of the people were
received in black velvet bags, suspended from hoops

attached to the end of long and well-rounded sticks. The first church was without spire or cupola, and the sound of a bell was never heard.

The old church, some ten years previous to its removal, was struck by lightning and considerably damaged. It was torn down in 1842 and all its materials disposed of, so that none of its remains is to be found in the present edifice. The old pulpit was purchased by Peter Woglom, and transformed into bee-hives, and a few of the old benches may still be found in different portions of Staten Island.

An object of considerable interest to those of antiquarian tastes is a small plane, long in the possession of the late Captain A. J. Wood, of Prince Bay, which was used for molding the boards first used in the construction of the original building.

But the most sacred of all relics, and held in trust by the pastor, is the old Bible, handled for half a century by the fathers of the church, who are now at rest with God. When William Lummis, father of the late Fletcher Lummis, was pastor here in 1830, he accidentally pushed, while preaching, this Bible from the desk, and in the effort to prevent it from falling wrenched the cover partly off. This episode accounts for the three strips of heavy leather on the back with which the damage was tolerably well repaired. The fly-leaf of this ancient volume bears the following inscription:

A Gift

from Nancy Dissosway to the

Methodist Church on Staten Island.

July 4t , 1795.

An old communion plate of German silver, used for many years in the first church, still survives the ravages of time.

At the next annual meeting, the first after the old church was dedicated, Abraham Cole and John Hillier were elected trustees for three years, and Nicholas La Forge was elected in place of Benjamin Drake, and John Morgan was elected to fill the vacancy on the removal of Joseph Wood from the Island.

During the first fifty years of this church, we find in the official board, as trustees and officers at the annual meetings, the following names of men prominent in their day for good works and valuable service to the church: Israel Dissosway, Gilbert Totten, John Slack, Andrew Prior, Jacob Rickhow, Peter Winant, Nicholas La Forge, Nicholas Crocheron, Joseph Totten, Peter Manee, James Totten, Wm. Cole, Edward Spragg, Jacob Rickhow, John Dubois, Isaac Cole, Abraham Cole the younger, James Guyon, John Totten, Abraham Auten, John Wood, Henry Rutan, Charles Androvette, Jacob Simonson, Cornelius Dissosway, Winant Winant and Jesse Oakley. On Aug. 2nd, 1844, the Rev. Henry Boehm, who had been elected trustee to fill the vacancy caused by the death of the Rev. Wm. Cole, offered his resignation, and Bornt P. Winant was elected to serve the unexpired portion of the term.

The old church having been taken down in 1842 the second and present edifice was erected on its site. It stands very nearly in the centre of the grounds. The building was completed late in the fall of that year, and dedicated on the 25th day of · December, Christmas Day, by the Rev. Charles Pitman, who also preached the sermon on this occasion. The new building was a great improvement on the old one, being more modern in the style of architecture, and was so located as to front on the road. The shorter windows of the former were exchanged for the longer and more churchly windows of the latter, and the gallery, instead of being on three sides, was limited to one, placed above the main entrances and forming a vestibule beneath. The projecting roof was supported by four massive columns, having a platform for a base, thus forming an outer portico; and these gave to the structure an air of impressiveness and quiet grandeur. All the lumber used in the foundation sills and for the support of the floor, in the present edifice, was most generously donated by the late John McNiesh.

At that time the following board of trustees was in office: The Rev. Wm. Cole, Winant Winant, Mark Winant, Isaac Winant, Cornelius Dissosway and Jesse Oakley.

The church cost $3,758.72. $2,108.72 of this was paid, leaving an indebtedness of $650. Altogether at that time the church was in debt $1,650.

In 1849, the Revs. Henry Boehm and Nicholas Vansant were appointed a committee to raise money by subscription to liquidate the debt then standing.

The tower, which cost about $750, was not added to the building until 1876, when a sweet-toned bell from the foundry of Meneely, West Troy, N. Y., weighing 1,525 pounds, and costing $550, was placed in position. This superb bell was presented by William Asbury Cole, of New York, grandson of the Rev. William Cole, of honored memory, and bears the following inscription:

A MEMORIAL OF
FANNIE H. COLE,
WHO DIED MAY 18th, 1876,

IN HER 13TH YEAR.

PRESENTED TO THE

WOODROW M. E. CHURCH,
BY HER PARENTS.

"UNTO YOU, O MEN, I CALL."

The following, among others, held positions in the official board between the years 1842 and 1896:

Wm. Cole,
Winant Winant,
Mark Winant,
Isaac Winant,
Cornelius Dissosway,
Jesse Oakley,
Eugene Halle,
John Cole,
Bornt P. Winant,
Peter L. Cortelyou,
Peter Woglom,
James J. Winant,
James Johnson,
Charles Androvette,

Israel LaForge,
Charles Bogardus, Sr.,
Charles Bogardus, Jr.,
John M. Sprague,
Andrew Eddy,
James S. Guyon,
R. Henderson Journeay,
James Eddy,
Wm. Butler,
Joshua Casscels,
N. A. Turner,
Edward Miller,
Peter E. Pearsall,
John P. Winant,

Edward Sprague.

The seal of the Society, inscribed with the words "Methodist Episcopal Church, Woodrow, S.I.," and designed for official documents, was adopted Feb. 6th, 1852, and is still in use.

In 1850 two acres of land, making nearly three acres now owned by the Society, were bought of Mr. A. R. Luyster for $400, for a parsonage site. The parsonage, located at the extreme west of the

grounds, was built the same year, during the pastorate of the Rev. Nicholas Vansant, though it never
proved a home to this estimable preacher, as his
ministerial term expired about the time of its completion. Its first occupant was his successor, the
Rev. Wesley Robertson.

The parsonage originally was half its present
dimensions, consisting of hall, sitting-room, dining-
room and bedroom on first floor, with rooms of
equal space above, and garret. The names of John
Cole and B. P. Winant appear as the building committee. In 1854, blinds were placed on all the
windows of the house, only the lower ones to this
time having had these desirable appendages, and
a small room annexed in the rear to the kitchen.
During the pastorate of the Rev. A. M. Palmer, 1860-
61, the building was enlarged nearly one-half, the
present parlor, rear hall and large rooms above being
added. The parsonage is now a most comfortable
and convenient one, plain in appearance, but exceedingly home-like and thoroughly furnished. It is
valued at $1,50c. The grounds adjoining are inclosed,
and sheds, barn and garden are at the disposal of
the pastor.

Recognizing the need of a suitable place for the
holding of fairs, festivals and other entertainments,
that these might be entirely excluded from the
church proper, the present frame building on the
east side of the property, known as the "Hall,"
was erected in 1884, at a cost of little more than
$900. Its dimensions are 25x50 feet, affording ample
room for all social gatherings, and it fully meets a
long-felt want. An annex 12x13 feet serves as a
kitchen, and chairs, tables, stoves, cutlery, glass-

ware and lumber enable the Society to prepare for
entertainments of any kind with but little incon-
venience.   The building stands as a monument to
the progressive spirit of the congregation during
the pastoral labors of the Rev. W. F. Randolph.

The burial ground is even older than the church
organization, sufficient room for interments being
secured at the time when the site for the first
house of worship was selected.   The cemetery at
the present time is supposed to contain upward of a
thousand graves.   A number of slabs are of brown
sandstone, the oldest of which bear respectively the
following names and dates:

Judith, wife of Paul Mersereau, 1767; Peter Poillon,
1780; Sarah Cairns, 1792; Martha Cairns, 1792; Isaac
Manee, 1794; Hannah, wife of Jacob Prior, 1795; James
La Tourette, 1796; Elizabeth, wife of Ephraim Johnson, 1797; Phebe, wife of Jacob Rickhow, 1798.

A large number of slabs, plain but neat, were
placed in position in the early half of the century,
and many more of costlier design have been erected
during the last half.   In several family plots may
be seen handsome monuments of marble or granite.

Up to the year 1781 New Jersey was all one charge
and Staten Island was under the care of the New
Jersey ministers.   The first apportionment of territory or division of charges was made at the conference held at Philadelphia, in June 1773.   In 1781,
New Jersey was divided into West Jersey and East
Jersey charges, and Staten Island was as a matter of
course included in East Jersey charge.   In 1786, Newark was formed into a separate pastorate and the
following year Elizabeth Town and Staten Island
were made a charge.

For many years thereafter Staten Island formed a part of what was then known as the Elizabeth Town district. In 1791, neither name appears in the minutes of the annual conference. In 1792-3, the Island stands alone, but the next year it again appears in connection with Elizabeth Town. From 1810 to 1815, it was a separate appointment. From 1815 to 1826, it formed a part of the district known as "Essex and Staten Island." From 1826 to 1839, it furnished a home and support for its own preachers, since which time it has been divided into smaller stations.

PASTORS.

NEW JERSEY.

1773—John King; William Waters.

1774—William Waters.

1775—John King; Daniel Ruff.

1776—Robert Lindsay; John Cooper.

1777—Henry Kennedy; Thomas McClure.

1778—Daniel Ruff.

1779—Philip Cox; Joshua Dudley; Daniel Ruff.

1780—William Gill; John James; Richard Garrettson.

EAST JERSEY.

1781—Caleb B. Pedicord; Joseph Cromwell.

1782—John Tunnell; Joseph Everett.

1783—Samuel Rowe; James Thomas; Francis Spry; William Ringold.

1784—Samuel Dudley; William Phoebus.

1785—Adam Cloud; Matthew Greentree.

1786—John McCloskey; Ezekiel Cooper.

ELIZABETH TOWN AND STATEN ISLAND.

1787—Robert Cloud; Thomas Morrell.

1788—John McCloskey; Simon Pile.

1789—John Merrick; John Cooper.

1790—Jethro Johnson; Gamaliel Bailey.

STATEN ISLAND.

1792—Thomas Ware.

1793—Thomas Everard.

ELIZABETH TOWN AND STATEN ISLAND.

1794—John Clarke; Hezekiah C. Wooster.

1795—S. Bostwick; R. Hutchinson; W. Storms.

1796—John Fountan; Albert Van Nostrand.

1797—John Clarke; T. Merritt; J. Seward.

1798—James Tolleson; Samuel Thomas; Thos. Morrell.

1799—Thomas Everard; David Bartine.

18cc—Joseph Totten; Jesse Justice.

1801-2—Joseph Totten; William Mills.

1803—Samuel Thomas; George Woolley; J. Stephens.

1804—Thomas Morrell; B. Iliff; Samuel Budd.

1805—Peter Van Nest; David Bartine.

1806—William McLenahan; David Bartine.

1807—James Moore; Jacob Heavener.

1808—James Moore; Thomas Stratton.

1809—William Smith; Thomas Stratton; J. Sharpley.

STATEN ISLAND.

1810—Thomas Drummond.

1811—Jacob Heavener.

1812—Sylvester Hill.

1813—John Robertson.

1814—James Polemus.

ESSEX AND STATEN ISLAND.

1815—Joseph Totten; John Robertson; Daniel Moore.

1816—Joseph Totten, John Potts, Daniel Moore.

1817—George Woolley, Edward Page.

1818—George Woolley, Richard W. Fetherbridge.

1819—Asa Smith, Bartholomew Weed.

1820—Asa Smith, Bartholomew Weed, James Long.

1821-2—Thomas Neal, Samuel S. Kennard.

1823—Lawrence McCombs, Isaac Winner.

1824-5—David Best, William A. Wiggins.

STATEN ISLAND.

1826-7—Bartholomew Weed.

1828-9—Benjamin Collins.

1830—William Lummis.

1831-2—John K. Shaw.

1833-4—Waters Burrows.

1835-6—Henry Boehm.

WOODROW.

1837-8—Mulford Day.

1839-40—Daniel Parrish.

1841-2—Wesley Robertson.

1843-4—Isaac N. Felch.

1845-6—James H. Dandy.

1847-8—Sedgwick Rusling.

1849-50—Nicholas Vansant.

1851—Wesley Robertson.

1852-3—Abraham Owen.

1854-5—Benjamin Kelley.

1856-7—Jacob P. Fort.

1858-9—John I. Morrow.

1860-61—Abraham M. Palmer.

1862-3—George Winsor.

1864-6—George W. Treat.

1867-8—Ambrose Compton.

1869-71—Jeremiah Cowins.

1872-4—Edward M. Griffith.
1875—Milton Relyea.
1876-7—Fletcher Lummis.
1878-80—Charles F. Hull.
1881-3—Isaac W. Cole.
1884-6—W. F. Randolph.
1887-89—E. S. Jamison.
189c-3—J. O. Winner.
1894—J. H. Timbrell.
1895—M. S. Lambert.

The Rev. E. S. Jamison in his book, "A Century of Life," gives the following account of the early ministers of the Island:

1787—Robert Cloud, Thomas Morrel. The latter was a major in the Revolutionary Army. In the battle of Long Island he was shot through the body with a British ball. His health failing, he retired from the army and repaired to his home in Elizabeth. He was converted when nearly forty years of age, under the preaching of the Rev. John Hagerty. His mind was turned soon after toward the ministry, and he was licensed to preach. He did much for Methodism in New York, and built, at the direction of the Conference, Forsythe Street Church, next in order of time to John Street. It was during his ministry here that the first church was erected. He died Aug. 9th, 1838, aged ninety years, eight months and seventeen days.

1788—John McClaskey, Simon Pile. Of the latter we know nothing. John McClaskey came to this country from Ireland when sixteen years of age. Loving the country of his adoption he served in her Revolutionary struggle, and at one time was a prisoner for a year in the old sugar-house. To escape

the ravages of yellow fever he writes that he went
into the country, but the spot in the country to
which he refers was that where Cooper Institute
and the Bible House in New York city now stand.
He was converted in 1782 and became an eloquent
preacher, a recognized leader and a wise counselor.
He died in 1814.

1789—John Merrick, John Cooper. The former
was a superior preacher, but located after eleven
years of great usefulness. The latter is described
as "a man of a solemn, fixed countenance," who
had suffered great persecution from his family. His
father, finding him upon his knees, threw over him
a shovel of hot embers, and finally drove him from
home. Such trials, however, left his faith unshaken.
He joined the company of traveling evangelists and
lived and died in their ranks.

1794—John Clark, Hezekiah C. Wooster. Wooster
was a most marvelous expounder of the Word.
His preaching was marked by an energy irresistible,
and "dwellers in the wilderness heard with amaze-
ment his overwhelming eloquence, and often fell in
their forest congregations like dead men." His
faith was Abrahamic and his prayers constant.
Such was the power of his influence and the unction
attending his words that while whispering his
exhortations, after consumption had impaired his
voice, men fell before him like soldiers shot on the
field of battle. His death occurred in 1798.

1796—John Fountain, Albert Van Nostrand. John
Fountain was ordained both deacon and elder by
Bishop Asbury. He was an intimate friend of Bishop
Coke and in early life the traveling companion of
the venerated Father Boehm. From an injury

received by the running away of his horse, he was obliged to locate, and settled at Matawan, N. J. He died in 1835.

1805—Peter Vannest, David Bartine. The first named was a personal friend of John Wesley. "A plain, practical preacher, thoroughly evangelical and more than ordinarily effective." In his ninety-second year he was observed going from house to house in Pemberton, N. J., where he lived, inquiring after the welfare of souls. His conversion was brought about through the earnest efforts of a Methodist class-leader by the name of Bundy.

1806—William McLenahan, David Bartine. The former was not only a fearless preacher of Christ, but was also distinguished for his loyalty to the government, and received from Washington a letter commending him for using his influence in favor of peace and the enforcement of law.

1807—James Moore, Jacob Hevener. One writes of the first: " His life was so holy that I felt an awe in his presence, and yet so winning, loving, and beautiful was his conduct that he drew all, even the hearts of little children, to him." The latter was smart, keen, relentless in his opposition to Calvinism, but died out of the Methodist Episcopal church.

1826-7—Bartholomew Weed, second term. A most honored, and faithful minister of Christ. He was born in Danbury, Conn., March 6th, 1793, and died in Newark, N. J., January 5th, 1879. An evidence of the estimation in which he was held by his brethren is shown by his election as a delegate from the Rock River Conference to the General Conference of 1844, held in the city of New York. For the last eleven years of his life he was chaplain of the Essex county jail in New Jersey.

1830—William Lummis, father of the late Fletcher Lummis. The entire membership of the charge at this time was 96. The family of this earnest preacher consisted, beside himself, of a wife and three children. He received for his year's work $196. As a contrast to this the present membership on the island is 1,962, with 93 probationers. There are eleven churches, paying their pastors in the aggregate $10,832.

1831-2—John K. Shaw. A man of culture, young, strong, thoroughly devoted to his work, and a most indefatigable worker. His ministry was marked by a wonderful revival. About three hundred persons were converted, most of whom united with the church.

1833-4—Waters Burrows. Three years later he was elevated to the office of presiding elder, and continued to serve the church in this new relation for eight years. In the administration of discipline he was judicious and kind, and not only commanded the respect of his brethren, but was the happy recipient of their fullest confidence. In 1855, he organized Hedding Church, Jersey City, and was its first pastor.

1835-6—Henry Boehm. The monument which marks his grave was unveiled June 8th, 1878, and was an occasion of great interest and solemnity.

1841-2—Wesley Robertson. His pastorate was distinguished by a most gracious revival, which added greatly to the strength of the Society both in numbers and financial ability, and was the initial to the present church edifice and also that of Bethel, at Tottenville, both of which were erected while he was preacher in charge. He died in Jacksonville, Florida, Nov. 2nd, 1864.

1843-4—Isaac N. Felch. A manly man and a good preacher. He toiled amid the sunshine and shadows of the itinerancy for half a century and for a time was presiding elder. He was the first appointed pastor to the present church edifice.

CENTENNIAL CELEBRATION.

At an official meeting held early in the month of June 1887, it was unanimously decided that, having reached the Centenary year in the history of the local church, it should be celebrated in such manner as was befitting so important an event. The pastor was appointed to take the matter into consideration and fix such time as in his judgment would be the most suitable. This he did, and subsequently recommended the first week in October, beginning with Sunday, the 2nd, and ending with Sunday, the 9th.

In view of the fact that it had been determined that no moneys, save the customary collections, should be asked for at any of the religious services, it was resolved that Friday and Saturday evenings of the jubilee week should be utilized for a fair and fete, in the hope that sufficient funds might be realized to pay a debt of $500 remaining on the Hall recently built, and make some necessary improvements. For this purpose a Ladies' Aid Society was organized, and the requisite preparations began with great enthusiasm and zeal.

The Centennial exercises began Sunday morning, Oct. 2nd. The church was elegantly decorated with century plants, ferns, autumn leaves and flowers. On the wall, in the rear of the pulpit, were suspended a portrait of Father Boehm and a large steel engraving of the "Ordination of Asbury," presented to the parsonage by the artist, Mr. Thomas Coke Ruckel, of Baltimore, Md. The old Bible which had been given to the church in 1795 occupied a conspicuous position on the reading desk. The sermon was preached by the Rev. O. A. Brown, D. D., of Hoboken, N. J. His theme was "The Invisibility of God," as suggested by St. John i, 18. The following hymn, written and dedicated to the church by the Rev. J. F. Dodd, pastor of Asbury Methodist Episcopal Church, New Springville, S. I., and secretary of the Newark Conference, was read by Dr. Brown and sung by the large congregation:

Our fathers' God, to Thee we raise
Our hearts this day in grateful praise,
For all thy love and mercy shown
To those whom here Thou long hast known.

A hundred years of toil and care
By honored saints, in faith and prayer,
Have brought thy constant blessing down
With good success their work to crown.

Thy word hath here been uttered long,
In sermon, speech, and joyful song,
By faithful men, with zeal and love,
With holy unction from above.

Its power, as of old displayed,
Hath many precious converts made;
Of whom some to this hour remain,
While others with the Master reign.

Now, gracious God, let blessings come
On this our old and honored home;
And, as the years flow on apace,
Endow her with abiding grace.

At the afternoon service, the pastor delivered his historical sermon, which, in accordance with a unanimous vote of the congregation, was preserved in printed form. In the evening the Rev. Dr. Freeman preached on "The Glory of Zion," from Psalms xlviii, 12, 13.   During the day fraternal letters were read, from Bishop J. F. Hurst, the Rev. J. N. Fitzgerald, D. D., the Rev. John S. Porter D. D., and Mrs. Mary Molyneaux, a daughter of Father Boehm.

The first in the series of reunion meeting with former pastors, continuing for four evenings, began on Monday night, when addresses full of happy memories and pleasing reminiscences were delivered by the Revs. J. Cowins, of Rahway, N. J., and A. S. Compton, of Ocean Grove, N. J.

On Tuesday evening the address was by the Rev. N. Vansant, of Chatham, N. J., who was kindly remembered and most heartily greeted by many old friends.   At the close of his remarks the Rev. J. F. Dodd, of New Springville, was introduced, who presented the greetings of Asbury Church, from which a large delegation was present with him.

On Wednesday evening the addresses were by the Revs. J. I. Morrow, of Newark, N. J., and C. F. Hull, of Bayonne, N. J.   Fraternal letters were read from the Rev. Milton Relyea, presiding elder in the New Jersey Conference, and the Rev. W. F. Randolph.

On Thursday evening the Rev. A. M. Palmer, of Woodbridge, N. J., addressed the meeting and was followed by the Rev. I. W. Cole, of Newark, N. J.   The Rev. Jesse Oakley, a local preacher, and identified with St. John's Methodist Episcopal Church at Rossville, S. I., was present, and also the Rev. J. G. Johnston, who presented the greetings of Kingsley Methodist Episcopal Church, of Stapleton, S. I., and the Rev. I. Vansant, who did likewise in behalf of the church at Pleasant Plains.   The service was appropriately closed with brief remarks from the Rev.

W. H. Sanford, of Belleville, N. J., a venerable brother nearly ninety years of age, who also pronounced the benediction; and thus ended this series of reunion meetings that from the first were full of interest and very largely attended.

Friday and Saturday evenings were devoted to the fair and fete, under the auspices of the Ladies' Aid Society. The Hall was tastefully decorated with bunting and the tables ornamented with flowers. In one corner, on a slightly raised platform, neatly partitioned with drapery, sat one of the oldest members of the church, Mrs. H. Journeay, familiarly known as "Aunt Abby," working away at a spinning-wheel, and thus recalling the day of "Auld Lang Syne." A round table more than two hundred years old stood in another corner and was covered with curiosities not less than one hundred years old.

A beautiful silk quilt, to be presented to the person who should succeed in collecting the largest sum of money, was awarded to Mrs. R. Simonson, who had received $126.61. Mrs. George Eddy collected $84.60 and Mrs. Samuel Barton $77.03.

A handsomely-crocheted and embroidered Afghan appealed to the taste and ambition of three other ladies, and was presented to Mrs. C. Bogardus, Sr., whose collections amounted to $100.50. Mrs. J. T. Casscles had secured $51.75 and Mrs. Edward Miller, $10.

The gross receipts from all sources amounted to $1,420.44; expenses, $208.31; so that the net profits to the church are $1,212.13. To this amount must be added the receipts from the sale of a few articles left on hand.

In token of valuable services rendered the pastor

and wife were made the recipients of several elegant gifts. The week's celebration was brought to a most successful close with the services of Sunday, Oct. 9th. In the morning the Rev. J. A. Roche, D, D., of Brooklyn, N. Y., preached from portions of Rom ix, 5; 1 Cor. iv, 7 and Heb. i, 1.

In the afternoon the Rev. S. F. Upham, D. D., professor in Drew Theological Seminary, preached from John iv, 38, and in the evening the Rev. S. Van Benschoten, D. D., presiding elder of the district, spoke on "Christ as the Morning Star," taking his text from Rev. xxii, 16, and thus ended, with a success far surpassing all expectation, that centenary celebration of the church toward which so many had looked with mingled hopes and fears.

On Jan. 9th, 1888, the trustees passed a resolution thanking Mr. Jamison for his services in carrying out so successfully the centennial services of the church in the previous October.

At a meeting of the trustees called April 13th, 1890, Charles Bogardus, church treasurer, reported that he had received a check, the amount of the legacy of O. A. Wood, for $2,553.65.

In 1890, the Rev. John O. Winner was appointed to Woodrow, and served a term of four years. The Rev. John O. Timbrell took his place in 1894 and served the charge for one year. Several were converted during the revival services held by him in the winter of 1895.

Repairs were made on the parsonage during his short term and furniture bought at a cost of $150.

At the annual session of conference, held on Staten Island, at Tottenville, April 1st, 1895, the Rev. Marcus S. Lambert was appointed to the Woodrow charge. Mr. Lambert's first work was to take into consideration the advisability of repairing the church building. After several meetings with the trustees, it was decided to remodel the church. Work was begun in September of that year. The contract for the metal ceiling and side-walls and the painting and decorating was given to a New York contractor, and the contract for painting the interior, for the sum of $600; the carpenter work was given out for $100, and the lumber was purchased for $100.

The Ladies' Aid Society furnished the church with pulpit chairs and carpeted the building at a cost of $175. A new Sunday-school room was fitted up, and the exterior of the building painted, at a cost of $275. The total cost of improvements was $1,200, nearly all of which was in hand by the opening day.

The church was re-opened on Nov. 17th, 1895, the Rev. Dr. McCowan delivering the morning sermon, and the Rev. Dr. Howard that of the afternoon.

Woodrow has a fine Sunday-school which is the oldest on the Island. C. C. Bogardus, Jr., is the superintendent, and has been for nearly twenty years. It has also a flourishing Epworth League, of which W. H. Bedell is president, and an efficient Ladies' Aid Society, Mrs. Israel Bedell, president.

These organizations are important factors in the spiritual and temporal prosperity of old Woodrow Church.

NOTE—For the greater portion of the facts contained in the above history of Woodrow M. E. Church, we are indebted to the Rev. E. S. Jamison's excellent book, " A Century of Life," issued in 1887.

In 1897, the Rev. Theodore D. Frazee was sent to Woodrow, and his pastorate, during the past year, has been eminently successful. The attendance at the services has increased, and many new scholars have been added to the Sunday-school. The minister's salary has been increased by $100, and all assessments for benevolent purposes have been fully paid up. The trustees are already making arrangements to make many needed improvements to the parsonage next year.

Among the former prominent and active members of the church, who have helped to its success with both time and money, are the following:

Mr. and Mrs. Peter L. Cortelyou.
"   George Merscreau.
"   N. A. Turner.
"   George W. Eddy.
"   J. S. Casscles.
"   John V. S. Woglom.
"   James J. Winants.
"   James Johnson.
"   Eugene Halle.
"   Cornelius Winant.
"   J. S. Guyon.
"   B. P. Winant.
"   Cornelius Disosway.
"   James Johnson.
"   John Cole.
"   Charles Androvette.
"   Lewis Androvette.
"   Daniel Sharrott.
"   Isaac Winant.
"   Locke Cortelyou.
"   Jesse Oakley.

Mr. and Mrs. R. Henderson Journeay.
    "   John D. Winant.
    "   Edward Sprague.
    "   John P. Winant.
    "   William Butler.
    "   George Eddy.
    "   Richard LaForge.
    "   Winant Winant.
    "   Mark Winant.
    "   Bornt Winant.
Miss Phebe Ann Swaim.
Mrs. James Moore.
   "   George Mersereau.
   "   Israel La Forge.
   "   William Casscles.
   "   William Luscomb.
   "   Moses Winant.
Mr. Andrew Eddy.

PRESENT OFFICIALS.

TRUSTEES:

Charles Bogardus, Sr., president; David L. Winant, treasurer; William H. Bedell, secretary; Charles Bogardus, Jr., committee on ways and means; James Eddy, Edward Miller, James Smith, A. R. Kelsey.

STEWARDS:

William H. Bedell, secretary; David L. Winant treasurer; James Smith, Charles Bogardus, Sr., Charles Bogardus, Jr., A. R. Kelsey.

Organist: Miss Eugenia Wincapaw.

LADIES' AID SOCIETY:

Mrs. Israel Bedell, president; Miss Julia Spafford, secretary; Mrs. D. L. Winant, treasurer.

SUNDAY-SCHOOL:

W. H. Middleton, superintendent; R. E. Mersereau, secretary; Miss Sadie Miller, treasurer; Mrs. R. E. Mersereau, teacher infant class; Miss Eugenia Wincapaw, organist.

EPWORTH LEAGUE:

W. H. Bedell, president; Walter Houseman, secretary and treasurer.

JUNIOR EPWORTH LEAGUE:

Miss Florence Frazee, president; Mrs. William H. Middleton, vice-president.

The present membership is 73, nearly all of whom are active, working members, helping the church with both time and money:

Mr. and Mrs. J. W. C. Englebrecht.
" Israel Bedell.
" William H. Bedell.
" Charles Bogardus, Sr.
" Charles Bogardus, Jr.
" Nelson Gilby.
" William Gray.
" Walter Houseman.
" Edward S. Miller.
" James H. Moore.
" Peter E. Pearsall.
" William Price.
" John M. Sprague.
" David L. Winant.
" James Smith.
" William H. Middleton.
" Edward Sprague.
Mrs. Robert W. Dixon, Jr.
" Richard Lunt.
" Harry Kelsey.

Mrs. George Brown.
   " Harriet Woglom.
   " Rebecca Winant.
   " Lydia Winant.
   " Rizpah Boehm.
   " Maria J. Blackwell.
   " Mary A. Fuentes.
   " Nellie Kelsey.
   " Mary J. Leavitt.
   " Mary Mersereau.
   " Caroline E. Sidle.
   " Elizabeth P. Mallett.
Miss Jane H. Cole.
   " Martha Douglas.
   " Teresa V. Douglas.
   " Adda Esselborn.
   " Mary E. Blackwell.
   " Adrietta Guyon.
   " Sarah Miller.
   " Sarah J. Walker.
   " Castilia Moore.
   " Henrietta Moore.
   " Julia F. Spafford.
Mr. James C. Pearsall.
   " Thomas Sprague.
   " Stephen B. Winant.
   " James Colon.
   " William Winant.
   " James S. Guyon.
   " Albert Houseman.
   " Abram R. Kelsey.
   " Cornelius C. Androvette.
   " John W. DePew.
   " James Eddy.

Mr. William Englebrecht.
" William D. Butler.

BETHEL M. E. CHURCH,

TOTTENVILLE, NEW YORK.

BETHEL, M. E. CHURCH.
Tottenville.

CHAPTER IV.

BETHEL.

BY THE REV. J. H. HOWARD, D. D.

BETHEL METHODIST EPISCOPAL CHURCH of Tottenville is the eldest daughter of Woodrow M. E. Church.

Among the early converts to Methodism was James C. Wood who resided in one of the five houses which then constituted what is now the village of Tottenville. In his house were held the first Methodist prayer-meetings, which were the nucleus out of which have grown the two large, flourishing churches of Bethel and St. Paul's.

Among his co-laborers in these early days of Methodism were Gilbert Totten, William Drake, Cornelius Sleight, Daniel Butler, Abram Johnson, Joseph Palmer and Wesley Robertson. The exact date of these first meetings cannot be ascertained, but they must have been begun in the latter part of the eighteenth century.

These meetings were held at the houses of the different members of the Woodrow church who resided in this portion of the town. Occasionally, the traveling preachers of the denomination preached in the Richmond Valley school-house, and in 1806 a service was held there by Mr. Asbury.

It was not until 1822 that this portion of the scattered congregation felt sufficiently strong, financially, to have a building of their own for public worship.

After considerable discussion of the matter it was at last decided to settle the question by a vote of the entire Woodrow congregation and for this purpose a meeting was called for Feb. 12th, 1822. Richard Jackson and James Totten were chosen presiding officers. A vote was then taken and it was resolved, by a unanimous vote, "to build a house for the use and purpose of public worship, to be denominated the Methodist Episcopal Church, or to distinguish it more properly from the others (Woodrow and the Neck Church, now Asbury), 'The Tabernacle.'"

A vote was then taken for trustees and the following were unanimously elected: John Totten and James C. Wood, first class; John LaForge and Peter Manee, second class; Henry Rutan and Henry Manee, third class; Wm. Cole, treasurer.

The site was given by Joseph Totten who owned a large farm at Richmond Valley. This site was on the north side of Amboy road, a short distance east of the old LaForge store.

The Tabernacle was built by James LaForge, of Pleasant Plains, and was a very plain building, about 25x35 feet, without any pretensions to ornament, with neither cornice nor steeple. The outside was sheathed with plain pine boards placed horizontally and overlapping like the modern siding; the inside was ceiled with wide pine boards, planed, tongued and grooved by hand. The seats were plain benches, made by the carpenter. There were two front doors,

the right-hand door for women only and the left-hand
door for the men.

The platform and pulpit stood between the doors,
in front of which was the aisle with pews on either
side, the right for the women and very small children and the left for men only.

Near the men's entrance were the stairs leading
to the gallery which ran along the left side of the
church only, over the men's pews.

A meeting was held in the Tabernacle on the 4th day
of August, 1823, to choose the first board of trustees
to take charge of the temporalities of said house
(as it was thought proper to make a new arrangement to commence from this date).

James C. Wood and John Totten were chosen by
a plurality of voices to compose the first class;
Henry Manee and Aaron Johnson, to compose the
second class; Peter Manee, the younger, and James
Palmer to compose the third class.

It is difficult for us, in these days of many churches,
good roads and abundant means of transportation,
to realize with what pride and satisfaction our pious
forefathers saw the completion of their plain, modest
little place of worship. For thirty-five years they
had had but one place of public worship in Westfield.

For thirty-five years they had traveled over
long rough roads, through storm and sun in summer, through snow and sleet and mud in winter
from Tottenville, Pleasant Plains, Rossville and all
the surrounding country, to hear the occasional
sermons of itinerant ministers.

We may readily believe then that the little Tabernacle was the result of much self-denial and sac-
rifice and that it seemed a fair temple to the simple

farmers of those days, and that the good mothers were greatly rejoiced that they had a convenient place of worship where they could go and take their young children.

They had been waiting thirty-five years to build a church which cost only what Bethel has recently given at a single collection for missionary purposes.

Many men and women who afterward became earnest, active workers in the church and helped in after years to make old Bethel one of the leading churches on the Island, were converted in the old Tabernacle which was the second place of public worship in the town of Westfield.

Among these, many of whom now sleep in the Bethel church-yard, were:

Mr. and Mrs. John Totten.		Mr. and Mrs. Joseph Palmer.	
"	Joseph Sprague.	"	Cornelius Sleight.
"	James C. Wood.	"	Henry Money.
"	M. S. Taylor.	"	John Manee.
"	Wm. W. Wier.	"	Abraham Sprague.
"	Henry Cole.	"	Cornelius Palmer.
"	Wm. H. Rutan.	"	James C. Totten.
"	Wm. C. Manee.	"	Aaron Johnson.
"	Ephraim J. Totten.	"	Peter Manee.
"	James Totten.	"	Winant Sleight.
"	Wm. C. DuBois.	"	John La Forge.
"	Wm. Manee.	"	Henry Manee.
"	Andrew Sprague.	"	James Sprague.
"	James Manee.	Mrs. Abby LaForge.	
"	Jacob Weir.	"	Hetty Bertine.
"	Thomas Butler.	"	Peter Disosway.

Of these, only three, Capt. James Sprague, James Manee, and Cornelius Sleight, are living at the present time.

At this time the services were conducted for the most part by the local class leaders and exhorters, the Rev. Benjamin Cole, the Rev. James C. Wood, the Rev. Elias Price and others. It is said of Mr. Wood that in mild weather, when the Tabernacle windows were open, people sitting on their porches at Pleasant Plains could plainly hear his stentorian voice. He was noted for his religous zeal, and many of the early Methodists of Bethel Church owed their conversions to his labors.

The Revs. Elias Price and Benjamin Cole were also devoted ministers and indefatigable workers in these early days and were powerful factors in the building up of the church.

During the fifty-one years from the time of the first services held in Peter Van Pelt's house in Rossville, in 1771, to the building of the Tabernacle in 1822, the number of preachers in America had increased from 10 to 1,000, and the membership from 1,000 to over 250,000. At this time and for many years afterward the Tabernacle and all the Methodist congregations of Staten Island depended for their services upon the local preachers, exhorters, class leaders and the ministers stationed at Elizabeth, N. J.

The ministers who had charge of Essex county, N. J., and the Tabernacle in 1822, were Thomas Neall and Samuel S. Kennard, and the following year they were succeeded by Lawrence Mc Combs and Isaac Winner. The full list of the preachers up to the time when the Bethel Church was made a separate charge will be found in the history of the Woodrow Church.

The Tabernacle was used about sixteen years, when the growth of the society made a larger place of worship necessary.

At a meeting held in the Tabernacle, June 1841, for the purpose of taking into consideration the ques-

tion of building a new Methodist Episcopal church,
it was unanimously resolved that a new church be
built, and that a new site be purchased for the
church and burying-ground.

John Totten, Sr., James C. Wood and the Rev.
Wesley Robertson were appointed a committee to
select the site and superintend the building of
the church thereon.

At a later meeting the committee reported that
they could obtain one acre of land of John Totten, Sr.,
situated a few rods west of his house on the public
road leading to Amboy ferry.

This offer was unanimously accepted and a committee authorized to purchase said lot and superintend the building of a house 40x50 ft.

On Oct. 27th, 1841, the first board of trustees was
elected to take charge of the new church.

The first class consisted of James C. Wood,
Ephraim J. Totten, Abraham C. Totten; second class,
Richard C. DuBois, Abram H. Wood, Henry Manee;
third class, Abram Sprague, James Sprague, John
Manee. James C. Wood was made president of the
board and Ephraim J. Totten secretary.

The new church was built by I. P. Bedell, nephew
of John LaForge, who built the old Tabernacle. The
new church was finished in the spring of 1841 and
dedicated by the Rev. Charles Pitman, who was
presiding elder of the district, under the name of
" B t el.' At this time the Rev. Daniel Robertson
was pastor of Woodrow and Bethel, both churches
remaining under one charge until 1849, when at
the request of the Quarterly Conference they were
given separate pastors.

The success of the Bethel congregation in build-

MRS. HANNAH DRAKE.
The oldest Member of Bethel.

ing what was then by far the finest Methodist
church on Staten Island seems to have inspired the
Woodrow and New Springville congregations to re-
newed efforts, for two years later the little Woodrow church gave place to the present place of worship and in 1850 the New Springville people built
a new brick church.

In 1849, the board of trustees was reduced to six
and was as follows: Henry Cole and James M. Rutan,
one year; E. J. Totten and James Butler, two years;
Wm. Wier and Wm. C. Manee, three years; Wm.
Wier, president, Henry Cole, secretary, and E. J.
Totten, treasurer. The same year Bethel was set
apart as a separate charge and the Rev. Mulford
Day was sent here as the first pastor of Bethel
Church.

On March 10th, 1850, E. J. Totten tendered his resignation as trustee and treasurer, on account of his
being about to leave for California.

In October 1850, the number of trustees was
increased to seven, and John DuBois was elected to fill
the vacancy caused by the resignation of E. J. Totten,
and John S. Journeay, Geo. H. Cole and Abraham C.
Totten were elected trustees for three years.

On the 22nd of July, 1851, at a meeting of the board
of trustees, the president, Wm. Wier, stated that the
business before the board was to take into consideration the propriety of purchasing a lot for
the parsonage, and on motion of the preacher in
charge, Mr. Fort, it was resolved "that in the
opinion of this board of trustees it will be expedient
to build a parsonage provided a suitable lot can be
procured." Wm. Wier, Henry Cole, John S. Journeay, Wm. H. Rutan and John Fort were appoint-

ed a committee to purchase the lot as soon as possible.

On Sept. 16th, 1851, Mr. Fort reported that the committee had purchased a lot from A. C. Totten for the sum of $200. This same year the old platform steps in front of the church were taken down and separate platform steps erected at each entrance. In 1852, a resolution was passed that a charge should be made for burying in the churchyard, of $2.00 for each resident, and $3.00 for each non-resident.

At a meeting held Jan. 11th, 1852, W. H. Rutan of the building committee of the parsonage reported that he had received from the trustees $700, and that there was due him from collections $2.94; that he had paid for said building $682.80, leaving a balance of $20.14 due the board. It appears that $510 of this amount had been borrowed from the Rev. John Fort, for which the trustees gave their note, payable the first day of May.

The first of the famous oyster suppers of Bethel Church, of which we have record, was in February 1852, and netted $275.10. The first trustees' meeting held at the new parsonage was on Aug. 8th, 1853. At this meeting a resolution was passed to complete the fence around the parsonage if sufficient money could be raised at a collection in the church and also that no lectures be given in the church without the consent of the preacher in charge.

It is presumed that the collection was insufficient to fence the parsonage grounds, for on June 6th, 1854, the receipts of the grave-yard, $55.50, were used for the erection of a fence.

In 1855, the church was repainted and the grave-

yard improved; a barn was also built on the parsonage lot.

It seems that it was the custom for the bearers
to fill in the graves, for in that year an additional
allowance was made to the sexton of 50 cents for
each adult and 25 cents for each child, for filling in
the graves.

In 1857, for the better accommodation of that
portion of the congregation living in the village of
Tottenville, a site was purchased from the heirs of
the Parkinson estate, where St. Paul's Church now
stands, and a brick chapel erected at a cost of
$3000. One service each Sunday was held in the
chapel, by the pastor of Bethel Church.

In 1857, the church was renovated and repaired
at a cost of $81.41. In October 1858, at a meeting of
the board of trustees it was reported that the ladies
had held a fair and had passed a resolution to cushion
the seats of the church from the proceeds of the fair,
after paying the bond of Mrs. Cole. The trustees
disposed of this in very few words, as follows:

"Resolved, that the seats be not cushioned. Resolved, that the money now on hand from the fair
and festival be paid over to the treasurer, Bro. Wm.
Wier."

It is evident that our forefathers had no idea of
having money squandered on such luxuries as pew
cushions, but we think they were a little incon-
sistent, as at the next meeting they decided to dis-
pense with the "hat," and purchase four collection
baskets.

This resolution against putting cushions into the
pews seems to have created no little stir among
the ladies, for at a subsequent meeting of the board

it was reported that the ladies would turn over
one-half of the money, provided they were allowed
to use the other half for the purpose of a communion service for the church, provided also that the
"resolution on the book" against cushioning the
pews, be stricken out. Peace was restored at last
by the trustees passing a resolution to purchase
the communion set themselves, allowing the ladies
to furnish cushions at any future time, by raising
the necessary funds.

On Dec. 16th, 1858, at an adjourned meeting, the
board of trustees was increased to nine.

It was not until 1858 that burial plots were sold in
the church-yard. At that time it was resolved to
sell them at $1.00 per foot, no person being allowed
to purchase more than 14 feet square, or one lot.
The proceeds of the sale of said lots were to be used
for extending and protecting the grave-yard. At
the next meeting of the trustees a resolution was
passed to purchase a lot of one and one-half acres
from E. J. Totten, for a burying-ground, for the sum
of $500.

The chapel congregation was not willing long to
remain dependent upon Bethel, and, in 1859, made
application to the quarterly conference to be set
apart as a separate charge and to make a fair
division of the church property. The conference
was willing to make the chapel independent and
give them the chapel, but no more.

This question was discussed for a time with a
good deal of feeling as may be inferred from the following resolution passed Dec. 21st, 1859:

"*Resolved*, That we, the trustees of this Bethel M
E. Church, holding the said church and parsonage

in trust, do hereby agree unanimously to refuse to transfer or relinquish all or any part of the said church and parsonage to the trustees of St. Paul's Church, or any other such board, under any circumstances."

The question was finally referred to the presiding elder and the annual conference and they decided that the chapel trustees should release all claim to Bethel Church, that the church trustees should release all claim to the chapel and pay to them such portion of the cost of the parsonage as the number of seceding members bore to those who remained with Bethel, and the whole matter was finally amicably settled in accordance with the above decision.

At a meeting of the trustees held on Jan. 23rd, 1860, a resolution was passed to make application to the conference for a preacher to serve Bethel only. E. J. Totten was requested to write to the presiding elder and to consult the members of the congregation, and to receive subscriptions for the support of a separate minister. It was also decided to consult the Rev. Mr. Kelly whether he would accept a call with the consent of the conference. On Oct. 1st, 1861, at a meeting of the members of Bethel Church, a resolution was unanimously passed that the membership of Bethel M. E. Church authorize the trustees of said church to quit claim to St. Paul's Church all right, title and interest in said church, and property belonging to said church, to the trustees of said church.

At a meeting of the trustees held April 22nd, 1861, a resolution was passed to improve the church by having it raised so that a basement could be put under it. The trustees were authorized to borrow the money for the same, and to give satisfactory security on the church property.

An addition of 20 feet deep was put on the front and a lecture and Sunday-school room was provided by raising the building 9 feet and putting in a basement story.

At a meeting held in the church Thursday evening, February 1862, to ake into consideration the subject of "lay delegation," the subject being presented by the Rev. Mr. Kelly, fifteen votes were cast in the negative and none in the affirmative.

In 1865, the church purchased of E. J. Totten a tent and shed, in what is known as Bethel grove, to be used for entertainments, festivals, etc.

In 1867, the pipe organ was put into the church, at the cost of $2,000, the old organ being given for $500 in part payment. At this time the alcove was built in the rear to make room for the organ, and new lamps and chandeliers were put in, at the cost of $125.

In 1870, O. H. Barnard presented the trustees with a communion service, the same that is now in use in the church.

On Feb. 25th, 1879, Philip A. Joline, Philip De-Waters and Mathew Reckhow, as committee on soldiers' monuments, requested the trustees to donate a piece of ground 15 feet square in front of the church, for the purpose of erecting a monument "in respect to those gallant men who lost their lives in the Civil war." The request was granted, and M. E. Taylor, W. A. Brown and John H. Spragg were appointed a committee to locate the lot, and the use of the church was tendered to the monument committee for the following Decoration day.

On Dec. 19th, 1881, at a meeting of the **trustees,** a resolution was passed directing the treasurer to pay off the mortgage of the church, held by J. J. Winant. The Rev. S. J. Morris and W. A. Brown were appointed a committee to draw up the document to be placed on the tree, to be read on Christmas Eve as a present to the congregation, congratulating them that their church was at last free and clear of debt.

At the same meeting a resolution was passed to purchase from E. J. Totten for $400, five acres more or less, joining the cemetery, to enlarge the same, provided the official board gave their consent. This consent was given at a meeting held Jan. 11th, 1882, and the property consisting of 5.80 acres was added to the cemetery. The official seal of Bethel Church was filed in the office of the county clerk on April 21st, 1883.

In 1884, the church was declared entirely out of debt, but in order to buy a piece of land back of the cemetery, now called the grove, the trustees mortgaged the church $4,000.

This same year, during Mr. Palmer's pastorate, a fair was held to raise money to repair the church. About $2,000 was realized from the fair and subscriptions.

The walls were repapered and frescoed, and the woodwork finished in walnut and the organ in mahogany. The ceiling was a light azure studded with stars and small gilt figures, with a heavy dark border. The new chandeliers were of gilt, with cut-glass lamps and ornamental globes, and were especially handsome. There were six in all, two of which had four lamps each, and the others three. New Brussels carpet was laid throughout, new rugs and chairs provided for the chancel and the cushions were covered with maroon rep.

Re-opening services were held July 20th, 1884. In the morning the Rev. N. Vansant, the senior in respect to appointment, of the former pastors of the church, dating from the time St. Paul's was founded, preached from Eph. 1, 22; 23. After the sermon the Rev. A. M. Palmer stated that the cost of repairs already made amounted to $1,366.95. Of this amount, $1,121.63 had already been raised, leaving a deficiency of $245.32. He also stated that other repairs would swell the amount to $300. $275 was quickly subscribed.

In the evening, the Rev. S. B Rooney, another of Bethel's former pastors, gave an able sermon. Another subscription was taken, swelling the amount to $325.

A "Kate Greenaway" fair was held Dec. 11th, 12th and 13th. The proceeds, after paying expenses, amounted to $717.

OLD BETHEL BURNED.

From the Staten Island Times Jan. 16th, 1886.

"'Bethel Church is burned to the ground.' This is the first thing which greeted our ears and the ears of nearly every resident of Tottenville on Monday morning, and a sadder looking lot of people it would have been hard to find than those generous people who have worked so hard and sacrificed so much through the past years to build, enlarge and beautify and furnish this church. Forty-five years ago

EPHRAIM J. TOTTEN,
Born 1806. Died 1891.
President Bethel Board of Trustees and Recording Steward
forty years.

the members of the old tabernacle at Richmond Valley built Bethel Church, a plain unpretending structure 40x60 feet. This, at the time, was considered a large church for the place and had ample room to comfortably seat the largest congregations which assembled in those days, but at the end of fifteen years the attendance had outgrown the capacity of the building and it was enlarged by building an addition 10 feet deep to the front and a lecture and Sunday-school room was provided by raising 9 feet and putting in a basement story. As the church grew, and prospered, the members felt the need of a larger organ and as the organ loft which they then had was not strong enough to support such an instrument, in 1862 they still further enlarged the church by building an addition of eighteen feet to the rear, finishing off the basement for a class-room for the infant class in the Sunday-school and the upper part to receive the new organ which was purchased at the cost of about $2,500. They now had the church 40x98 feet, two stories high and with sufficient room to accommodate a large congregation for many years to come. The next work of the officers and congregation of the church was to pay off the debt, and this was accomplished in 1882 when the trustees made the church a present of a satisfaction of all its indebtedness.

"They now set to work to perfect the building erected at so great a cost, by decorating and beautifying the walls, purchasing new carpets and chandeliers, handsome chairs for the pulpit and last of all, a large and expensive heater for warming the building. In these improvements no less than $2,000 were expended, and to raise this sum

without incurring any indebtedness the ladies
of the church and congregation worked almost
incessantly for three years. In this work they
were aided by the hearty co-operation of their
sister churches and the public generally and about
two months ago the work was completed by the
purchase of a large new heater, and Bethel congregation felt they had done well and could now fully en-
joy their beautiful place of worship; and it was noted
last Sunday morning that the pastor, the Rev. A.
M. Palmer, seemed to take especial delight in the
handsome decorations and furniture and on his return home he remarked to his family that he did
not know a handsomer village church than Bethel.
At twelve o'clock that night all this was only a heap
of smoking ruins and all that was left was one little
organ and two small chairs.

" The fire is supposed to have taken from the new
heater and to have taken early in the day and
smouldered until late at night when it broke out.
The building and furniture were a total loss, nothing of value being saved.

" The total insurance was $8,525, $4,000 of which
was in the Richmond County Mutual Insurance Co.,
and $4,525 in the Glens Falls Insurance Co.

" It is estimated that about $20,000 had been ex-
pended on the church, but much less than that would
replace it, although it will cost probably double the
amount of the insurance.

" The trustees of St. Paul's M. E. Church, of the
South Baptist Church, and St. Mark's, of Pleasant
Plains, have kindly tendered to their homeless
brethren of Bethel the free use of their churches
and extend to them their sincere sympathy.

"Notwithstanding the heavy loss, made more distressing by the fact that they had just completed the work of improving and beautifying the edifice, the people are beginning, with good courage, to talk of rebuilding.

" The heat of the burning building and the falling of walls broke or chipped a number of the headstones nearest the church. Among those broken were the headstones erected to the memory of the following-named persons:

" Fanny H., widow of Jos. W. Totten, died 1866; Abram Sprague, died 1861, and his wife, Mary Sprague, died 1855; John Totten, 1846; Jas. Totten, 1879; Ann Amelia DuBois, 1849; Isabel Matilda DuBois, 1853; Rachel Jane DuBois, 1858; Mary Ann DuBois, 1875; John DuBois, 1860; John B. Cole, 1847; Henry Cole, 1854.

"Two monuments were also damaged: John L. Lenhart's, after whom Lenhart Post was named, being chipped and part of the inscription badly defaced, while the other, Willard E. W. Kent's, was thrown down and broken.

SISTER CHURCHES TO THE RESCUE.

" At a full meeting of the board of trustees of St. Paul's Methodist Episcopal Church, held on Monday evening, Jan. 11th, 1886, it was unanimously resolved:

" *First*, That we have heard with deep feeling of the very serious disaster which has befallen the Bethel Methodist Episcopal Church, of Tottenville, in the loss of its beautiful house of worship by a fire that has totally destroyed that old and honored landmark, and that we hereby express the Christian sympathy of the St. Paul's Methodist Episcopal Church with our sister society in its hour of sore disaster.

" *Second*, That the pews of the St. Paul's Methodist Episcopal Church are hereby declared free for the present and that the pastor and congregation of the Bethel Methodist Episcopal Church are affectionately invited, with the cordial concurrence of our pastor, to occupy with us the St. Paul's pulpit and building as long as our sister society may desire.

" *Third*, That a copy of these resolutions be sent to the pastor and official brethren of the Bethel M. E. Church and also to the *Westfield Times*.

JAMES W. SPRAGUE, President.

H. L. SPRAGUE, Secretary."

On Jan. 20th, 1886, a meeting was held at the parsonage to take preliminary measures toward building a new church. It was agreed to build at once or as soon as the work could be properly accomplished. The church was to be on the site of the former building, to be built of brick, and with certain improvements to make it both modern and attractive, and convenient. The Rev. A. M. Palmer, Peter Androvette and W. A. Brown were appointed a committee to examine suitable plans and report to the board of trustees.

Collectors were appointed to solicit subscriptions, and at a meeting held Feb. 1st, 1886, collections were reported amounting to $1,339.12, of which $532.11 had been paid in cash.

On the first Sunday in April of this year, the Rev. A. M. Palmer preached his farewell sermon. This was greatly regretted by the congregation, as it was believed that no new minister could render the same service during the coming year in the rebuilding of the church. It was hoped that some arrangement could be made with the conference by which Mr. Palmer could remain and finish the work he had begun with so much interest—that of re-building old Bethel, but at the session of conference Mr. Palmer was appointed to Woodbridge, N. J., and the Rev. J. R. Runyon, of that place, was his successor.

On May 5th, the bids for the new building were opened. Mr. McKeon, of Woodbridge, for the mason work, and Mr. Johnson, of Mount Loretto, for the carpenter work, were the lowest bidders. At a meeting held the next evening the trustees author-ized the committee to accept these bids.

The corner-stone was laid June 26th, 1886. The services were held in the grove. Among the minis-ters present were the Rev. J. N. Fitzgerald, D. D., of New York; the Rev. J. W. Ryder, the Rev. I. N. Vansant, the Revs. J. G. Johnston, T. E. Gordon and W. F. Randolph. After the services in the grove the meeting adjourned to the church where the Rev. J. N. Fitzgerald made an address and laid the corner-stone according to the ritual of the Meth-odist Episcopal church. Among the articles depos-ited by the pastor, the Rev. J. H. Runyon, in the stone, were the following: New Testament; dis-cipline of the church; copy of the Illustrated Sketch Book of Staten Island for 1886; copy of the *Staten Island Times*, Jan. 16th, 1886, containing the account of the burning of the church, and June 26th, 1886; *Westfield Independent* of June 26th; *Christian Advocate* of June 24th, 1886; minutes of Newark Annual Conference for the same year; constitution and by-laws of Richmond County Relief Association;

constitution and by-laws of Huguenot lodge, F. and A. M., of Tottenville; the names of the officers of Bethel Church; envelope from J. M. Androvette; a short history of the church, prepared by William M. Reid; a number of small silver coins and one of copper. At the meeting a collection was taken which, including four subscriptions taken a few days previous, amounted to $1,200.

The dedication services took place Sunday morning May 8th, 1887, in the presence of a large congregation. Bishop Harris performed the dedication service and the sermon was delivered by the Rev. Dr. Fitzgerald, now bishop.

After the sermon E. J. Totten, as president of the board of trustees, presented the church to the bishop, who then dedicated it according to the form of the Methodist Episcopal church. Services were also held in the afternoon, with preaching by the Rev. Dr. Chadwick, and in the evening the Rev. Dr. Van Benschoten, the presiding elder, occupied the pulpit. At the morning service the sum of $700 was raised and at the afternoon service this amount was increased to $1,000. In the evening $300 additional was subscribed to an organ fund.

The following report of the building committee was read:

"Amount of insurance received, $8,500, mortgage and interest paid, $4,25c, leaving a cash balance on hand when the committee began to build this church of $4,250.

" We have borrowed on bond and mortgage $6,000, we have received from the people more than $5,000, making in all $15,250. Our church as it stands has cost us $15,800 and will cost about $75 more;

so that we are now in need of $625 to pay all bills and finish what little work is yet necessary to be done.

"We desire to say that our people and friends have done nobly in giving and raising funds and we would acknowledge the following generous gifts:

"Our Sunday-school collected the money for the handsome front window.

"Sister A. C. Totten, of Jersey City, gave us the pulpit furniture and Brother E. J. Totten's sons, W. W. and James (through his widow), the pulpit.

"The Rev. J. W. Ryder and sister presented the Bible and hymn-book. Kreischer Brothers presented us with a fine bell, weighing about 1,400 lbs., as a memorial of their father, the late Balthasar Kreischer.

"There has been but little subscribed that has not been paid, so that we have been enabled to pay our obligations when they fell due. We trust, after to-day, to pay the balance that we owe and also to finish the church."

In 1889, in the pastorate of the Rev. W. B. Wigg, a new organ was purchased of Wm. H. Davis Bros., of New York, at a cost of $2,000. The money was raised by subscription.

Little of historical interest has occurred in Bethel Church since the new organ was purchased. In 1890, the legacy from the estate of O. A. Wood was received and $2,500 of the bonded indebtedness was paid off, leaving a balance of $3,500. Three years ago the trustees subscribed for twenty shares of the Richmond County Mutual Building and Loan Association, and when this matures it will more than pay off the mortgage and leave the property free of debt,

In 1895, the Rev. M. L. Gates, who was sent to Bethel by the conference, exchanged charges with the Rev. J. H. Howard, D. D., of Asbury M. E. Church, Wilmington, Del., and Dr. Howard served out that year and 1896, when he was succeeded by the present pastor, the Rev. Richard Johns. In 1895, the annual conference was held in Bethel Church, Bishop Hurst presiding.

BETHEL'S PASTORS.

Below we give the names and date of service of the different pastors, who have been appointed to Bethel Church since it was set apart from Woodrow M. E. Church, as a separate charge:

1841-2—Wesley Robertson, died at Jacksonville, Fla., Nov. 2nd, 1864, aged 57 years; 29 years in ministry.

1843-4—Isaac N. Felch, died at Hackettstown, N. J., March 24th, 1876, aged 69 years; 45 years in ministry.

1845-6—James H. Dandy, died at Rahway, N. J., May 12th, 1882, aged 84 years; 56 years in ministry.

1847-8—Sedgwick Rusling, died at Lawrence, Pa., May 7th, 1876, aged 77 years; 50 years in ministry.

1849-50—Mulford Day, died at Hackettstown, N. J., June 26th, 1851, aged 50 years; 18 years in ministry.

1851-2—John Fort, died at Blackwoodstown, N. J., Aug. 7th, 1875, aged 59 years; 33 years in ministry.

1853-4—Henry B. Beegle, died at Ocean Grove, N. J., March 20th, 1882, aged 71 years; 34 years in ministry.

CAPT. JOHN MILTON ANDROVETTE,

Local Preacher. Member of Bethel Church for the past thirty two years.

1855-6—John I. Morrow, supernumerary, residence at Newark, N. J.; entered ministry 1846.

1857-8—Charles S. Coit, died at Irvington, N. J., March 6th, 1898, aged 76 years; 51 years in ministry.

1859-60—John S. Swaim. died at Jacksonville, Fla., Nov. 18th, 1875, aged 69 years; 41 years in ministry.

1861—Benjamin Kelley, died at Port Jervis, N. Y., Oct. 24th, 1874, aged 60 years; 32 years in ministry.

1862-3—Nicholas Vansant, supernumerary, residence at Madison, N. J.; entered ministry 1842.

1864-5—E. W. Adams, residence at Aurora, Ill., Rock River conference.

1866-8—J. S. Chadwick, D. D., residence in Brooklyn, N. Y.; New York East conference.

1869-70—S. B. Rooney, supernumerary, residence in Buffalo, N. Y.; entered ministry 1845.

1871-3—I. N. Vansant. died at Stony Point, N. Y., Dec. 27th, 1897, aged 67 years; 39 years in ministry.

1873-6—H. D. Opdyke, stationed at Martinsville, N. J.; entered ministry 1863.

1877-9—Cornelius Clark, supernumerary, residence at Dover, N. J.; entered ministry 1857.

1880-1—S. J. Morris, moved from conference.

1882—H. C. McBride, New York East conference.

1883-5—A. M. Palmer, supernumerary, residence in Newark, N. J.; entered ministry 1842.

1886-8—J. H. Runyon, died at Tottenville, N. Y., Jan. 19th, 1888, aged 54 years; 32 years in ministry.

1889-91—W. B. Wigg, stationed at Paterson, N. J.; entered ministry 1865.

1892-4—Frederick Bloom, stationed at Newark'
N. J.; entered ministry 1874.

1895—M. L. Gates, moved from conference.

1895-6—J. H. Howard, D. D., stationed at Elizabeth,
N. J.; entered ministry 1882.

1897—Richard Johns, present pastor; entered ministry 1860.

FORMER MEMBERS.

Among those who have served in one or more
of the official boards of Bethel Church, or have been
active in advancing her material and spiritual
growth, the following deserve special mention:

Mr. and Mrs. Ephraim J. Totten.
"   Abraham C. Totten.
"   Abraham Sprague.
"   James W. Sprague.
"   John P. Manee.
"   Richard C. Du Bois.
"   William H. Rutan.
"   James Butler.
"   William C. Manee.
"   John S. Journeay.
"   John Du Bois.
"   Daniel Moore.
"   Aaron Van Name.
"   Joseph W. Sprague.
"   John Cole.
"   Shotwell B. Sprague.
"   James Sleight.
"   Henry Van Name.
"   Daniel Butler.
"   Isaac P. Bedell.
"   Abraham Cole.
"   E. P. Wood.

Mr. and Mrs. Henry D. Romer.
   "   Edward Decker.
   "   Andrew Sprague.
   "   M. S. Taylor.
   "   Johnson Sprague.
   "   Phillip B. Totten.
   "   Martin L. Joline.
   "   James Graham.
   "   William Lamond.
   "   Abram Price.
   "   William Manee, Sr.
   "   Thomas Butler.
   "   Cornelius Shea, Sr.
   "   Jacobson Wood.
   "   William Weir.
   "   S. W. Cronk.
   "   Joseph T. Polhemus.
   "   Jacob Wares.
   "   Richard La Forge.
   "   Charles H. Brown.
   "   James C. Davidson.
   "   John H. Graham.
   "   Samuel Sidell.
   "   J. W. J. Sprague.
   "   A. W. Joline.
   "   Peter Winant.
   "   F. B. Taylor.
Mrs. Hannah Drake.
Mr. James W. Sleight.
 " James C. Wood.
 " E. R. Bennett.
 " James M. Rutan.
 " George H. Cole.
 " Apka B. Ward.

Mr. C. M. Turner.

" Alfred H. Taylor.

" John Romer.

" John V. Romer.

" Elias Price.

PRESENT CHURCH OFFICIALS.

TRUSTEES:

Peter Androvette, president; John E. LaForge, treasurer; Richard Firth, secretary; Wm. A. Brown, Sr., superintendent of cemetery; Alfred H. Sprague, Theo. Jobes, Jas. W. Bedell, Geo. F. Reckhow, Eugene B. Halle.

STEWARDS:

Wm. E. Joline, secretary; Fernando W. Brown, treasurer; John M. Androvette, district steward; William Manee, Horatio Collins, James N. Depew, Geo. M. Totten, Charles Ainsworth, James A. Androvette, James H. Wood, Anderson Fisher, Zachariah Graham, A. Wesley Androvette.

Local preacher, George Okeson.

LADIES' AID:

Mrs. Jas. W. Bedell, president; Mrs. Alfred H. Sprague, vice-president; Mrs. Geo. M. Totten, secretary; Mrs. George W. Moore, treasurer.

SUNDAY-SCHOOL:

Wm. E. Joline, superintendent; Geo. F. Reckhow, assistant superintendent; Miss Ida M. Ryder, female assistant superintendent; Martin L. Fisher, secretary; Geo. Sprague, assistant secretary; John M. Androvette, treasurer; David E. Ryder, librarian; Jones Powell, Frank Wood, Henry Walling, assistant librarians; Miss Hattie Burgess, pianist; Miss Julia Jobes, Miss E. Blanche Brown, assistant pianists.

The superintendents who have served Bethel

CAPT. PETER ANDROVETTE
President Bethel Board of Trustees.

Sunday-school, since its organization, are appended, in their order. We are unable to give the terms of office of the first six superintendents, as the records containing these names were destroyed in the fire.

The list follows:

James Wood, Henry Cole, E. R. Bennett, Andrew Sprague, William Henry Rutan, Ephraim J. Totten, S. W. Cronk, 1860-70; William A. Brown, Sr., 1870-6; J. H. Graham, 1876-8; John M. Androvette, 1878-82; David M. Sprague, 1882-6; James H. Christopher, 1886-9; David M. Sprague, 1889-91; James H. Christopher, 1891-2; William E. Joline, 1892-8.

William A Brown, Sr., is the oldest living ex-superintendent.

EPWORTH LEAGUE OFFICERS:

George Okeson, president; Geo. M. Totten, first vice-president; Mrs. Howard Sprague, second vice-president; Miss Carrie Price, third vice-president; Miss Mineola Marshall, fourth vice-president; Miss E. Blanche Brown, secretary; Wm. Manee, treasurer; Miss Hattie Burgess, pianist.

The Epworth League was organized May 11th, 1891, under the name of Bethel chapter, No. 6265. It started with 29 members, which number has been increased to 126.

The first officers were D. M. Sprague, president; John C. Hall, first vice-president; Mrs. C. A. Joline, second vice-president; T. C. Totten, third vice-president; Mrs. Horatio Collins, fourth vice-president; B. F. Joline, secretary; W. E. Joline, treasurer.

PRESENT MEMBERSHIP.

The present membership is 256, as follows: Mr. and Mrs. Isaac P. Bedell.

Mr. and Mrs. James A. Androvette.
      "   Fernando Brown.
      "   Peter Androvette.
      "   James Ayr.
      "   William T. Abbott.
      "   John M. Androvette.
      "   Daniel B. Bedell.
      "   James W. Bedell.
      "   Henry Christopher.
      "   James H. Depew.
      "   Anderson Fisher.
      "   Richard Firth.
      "   Zachariah Graham.
      "   Truman Joline.
      "   Theodore D. Jobes.
      "   Richard LaForge.
      "   John E. LaForge.
      "   Peter Miller.
      "   William Lee.
      "   William Mance.
      "   David Price.
      "   Crowell Price.
      "   William Wood.
      "   Alfred H. Sprague.
      "   George F. Reckhow.
      "   George W. Slaight.
      "   David M. Sprague.
      "   William Sprague.
      "   George M. Totten.
      "   David F. Van Pelt.
      "   David Wares.
      "   Oliver Weir.
            Benjamin Weir.
      "   James H. Wood.

Mr. and Mrs. Charles M. Ainsworth.
     "   Reuben W. Androvette.
     "   A. W. Androvette.
     "   Wallace E. Bedell.
     "   James Bailey.
     "   Luther Boyce.
     "   Mulford C. Drake.
     "   George W. DuBois.
     "   Edward Gibson.
     "   Charles Johnson.
     "   William W. Jacklin.
     "   Robert Lee.
     "   Abram Latourette.
     "   John H. Price.
     "   F. C. E. Peterson.
     "   Amos A. Slaight.
     "   George F. Sorsby.
     "   William Spinola.
     "   William Decker.
Mrs. John Creighton.
   "   Richard Johns.
   "   William Taylor.
   "   David Wood.
   "   Wesley Wood.
   "   H. R. Yetman.
   "   George Wood.
   "   John Yetman.
   "   Alfred Storer.
   "   Charles Sickles.
   "   Wesley Totten.
   "   Hiram Reid.
   "   William Slaughter.
   "   Henry Stiles.
   "   Howard Sprague.

Mrs. William Moore.
" John Potter.
" George W. Moore.
" Jonah Manee.
" John Lake.
" A. J. Smith.
" Charles Lehman.
" William Journeay.
" Herman Dunham.
" George Creighton.
" William Butler.
" Samuel Brehaut.
" David Butler.
" Phebe Androvette.
" Mary A. Butler.
" Anna M. Cole.
" Ella M. Cooper.
" Elizabeth Corsen.
" Rebecca Daggett.
" Ann Decker.
" Carrie S. Dunham.
" Jane S. Hugett.
" Cecelia Joline.
" Mary E. Johnson.
" Ann M. LaVere.
" Jane M. Moore.
" Mina Manee.
" Ellen H. Ryder.
" Isabelle Gerry.
" Mary Arles.
" Almira Ryder.
" Sarah Polhemus.
" Cora B. Price.
" Frances J. Price.

Mrs. Sarah A. Shea.
   "   Mary J. Shea.
   "   Catharine J. Sprague.
   "   Sarah A. Springstead.
   "   Margaret Robbins.
   "   Mary J. Reid.
   "   Margaret Reckhow.
   "   Emma J. Sprague.
   "   Mary A. Toland.
   "   Mary E. Tyson.
   "   Jane Wares.
   "   Mary F. Wood.
   "   Mary H. Corson.
   "   Hannah Drake.
   "   Elizabeth Drake.
   "   Martha Dissosway.
   "   Nellie Decker.
Miss Mary W. Dissosway.
   "   Mary L. Dissosway.
   "   Emma S. Drake.
   "   Anna M. Weir.
   "   Josephine Wood.
   "   Mattie S. Wood.
   "   Mary Yetman.
   "   Inez A. Yetman.
   "   Minnie Sterling.
   "   Anna M. Totten.
   "   Nettie Totten.
   "   Laura B. Yetman.
   "   Fannie B. Reid.
   "   Bertha N. Reckhow.
   "   Maggie Mercer.
   "   Lena Messener.
   "   Carrie Price.

Miss Hattie Price.
  "   Jennie E. Peterson.
  "   Ida M. Ryder.
  "   Hannah E. Miller.
  "   Ella C. Miller.
  "   Samantha Manee.
  "   Susie Marshall.
  "   Minnie Marshall.
  "   Ida Winant.
  "   Ida B. Marshall.
  "   Ella S. LaForge.
  "   Addie E. Lake.
  "   Mamie A. La Forge.
  "   Nellie Joline.
  "   Maud DuBois.
  "   Mattie B. Dunham.
  "   Fannie B. Davis.
  "   Carrie Gibbs.
  "   Sadie Boyce.
  "   E. Blanche Brown.
  "   Nora Bailey.
  "   Mamie T. Collins.
  "   Ida S. Butler.
  "   Anna S. Butler.
  "   Clara Androvette.
  "   Mary E. Butler.
  "   Ida Winant.
  "   Ella Butler.
  "   Helen B. Johns.
  "   Charlotte Johns.
  "   Elizabeth Decker.
  "   Mary Cooley.
Mr. Horatio Collins.
  "   William M. Bedell.

Mr. Daniel Bedell.
    Andrew Abrams.
" William M. Carpenter.
" William A. Brown, Sr.
" John Gerry.
" Eugene B. Halle.
" William Joline.
" William E. Joline.
" Adelbert Price.
" Abram E. Price.
" James W. Manee.
" Ferdinand Peterson.
" Christian Peterson.
" William M. Ryder.
" David E. Ryder.
" J. W. Ryder.
" Joseph B. Collins.
" William Matthews.
" Herman F. Muller.
" George Okeson.
" Nelson Okeson, Jr.
" Andrew M. Sprague.
" William J. Sprague.
" Jesse R. Slaight.
" George Sprague.
" George M. Reckhow.
" James W. J. Sprague.
" Benjamin F. Joline.
" Olin C. Joline.
" Harry H. Joline.

PAUL'S M. E. CHURCH,

TOTTENVILLE, NEW YORK.

ST. PAUL'S M. E. CHURCH.
Tottenville.

CHAPTER V.

ST. PAUL'S METHODIST EPISCOPAL CHURCH, of Totten-ville, is an outgrowth of Bethel, and ,was organized by those members living in the village and who de-sired a more convenient place of worship.

A public meeting was called in 1856, during the pastorate of the Rev. John I. Morrow, of all persons interested in building a new church. After consid-erable discussion, a vote was taken and it was unanimously decided to begin at once and raise money to purchase a site and erect a church, or chapel, as soon as sufficient money could be raised.

The people took up the work with great energy, and by means of fairs, festivals and a sinking fund subscription, had raised enough within little more than one year to undertake the building of a small house of worship.

The first entry of cash received for the new chapel, on the books of the treasurer, is $414.30, the proceeds of a Fourth of July festival in 1856, and on the twentieth of the month the Rev. John I. Morrow turned in $158 collected on subscriptions, and by Sept. 11th, 1857, there was a balance in the treasury of over $700 after paying for a site 100x250 feet, where the church now stands, purchased August 10th, 1857, from the heirs of the Parkinson estate for $400. In November of that year, 135,000 bricks were purchased at $3.00 per thousand, and placed on the lot.

In 1858, during the pastorate of the Rev. C. S. Coit, the first board of trustees to take charge of the property, and erect a church, was elected at a meeting held Sept. 25th, at the house of David Joline, and consisted of the following: Abram Sprague, president; Wm. H. Totten, secretary; David Joline, treasurer; Wm. H. Rutan, James Butler, James W. Sprague, James M. Rutan, William Lamond and David Van Name.

The following year, 1859, the trustees made preparations to build a chapel 25x50 feet, and having received an offer from Huguenot lodge, F. & A. M., that if they would build it two stories high, the lodge would lease the second floor as a lodge-room for five years, at an annual rental of $75, the offer was accepted. The Masons retained this room for nearly twenty-five years and until, in remodeling the building for a Sunday-school room, the second floor was removed.

The contract for building the chapel was awarded in June 1859, the carpenter work to W. J. Shea, and the mason work to W. Burbank, the work being done by the day and the trustees furnishing all the material.

Soon after the commencement of the work, it became a question with the trustees whether or not the organization of a separate congregation or society, was necessary, in order to perpetuate the board of trustees. The law required the election of three trustees annually; and that they should be elected by the members of the congregation. The trustees were incorporated under the name and title of the "Trustees of the St. Paul's M. E. Church;" the conditions of the deed which they held stipulated that they were to hold the premises for the use of "the members of the St. Paul's M. E. Church," but there existed no membership of such church to whom they were amenable for the proper discharge of their duties, or by whom the statutory elections could take place so as to perpetuate the board, as the people who were interested in the work still retained their membership at Bethel.

The Rev. Mr. Swaim applied for advice to the Rev. J. S. Porter, presiding elder of the district, and to Bishop James, who suggested to him that as preacher in charge of Bethel station, it was competent in him to recognize the wish of any member, or members, of Bethel, to be transferred to the St. Paul's society, who would thenceforth, by virtue of such transfer, be known according to the usage of the Methodist Episcopal church, as members of the St. Paul's society. Agreeably with this suggestion, sixty-nine persons having signified such a wish, they were duly transferred; and the requirement of a membership contemplated by the charter given to the trustees, was complied with.

Work on the chapel was pushed forward rapidly, and on the 16th day of October, 1859, it was formally dedicated, in a sermon preached by the Rev. Mr. Swaim, from Isaiah 60,7, " I will glorify the House of my Glory."

After the dedication of the chapel Mr. Swaim held

the pastorate over both charges, and the morning service was held in St. Paul's and the afternoon service in Bethel. A prayer-meeting was held in both places, the preacher alternating in his attendance between the two.

Before the close of the year, it was found that this arrangement would give offense to some of the members of the Bethel society, and a feeling of disapprobation arose which ripened into a formal protest at the fourth quarterly conference held in March 1860, and the offering of a resolution asking the bishop at the ensuing conference for a preacher who should confine his labors in the pulpit to the Bethel Church exclusively, which resolution passed by a majority of one, the pastor declining to vote.

The members of St. Paul's, thus denied the privilege of sharing in the services of the pastor of Bethel Church, had no alternative left them but to apply to the conference to set apart St. Paul's as a separate charge. A public meeting of all friendly to such a measure was called for Monday evening, March 12th, and a large congregation, which filled the chapel, unanimously decided to present a petition to the bishop to be made a separate charge, and that the Rev. John S. Swaim be returned to them as their preacher.

At the conference held at Hackettstown, N. J., April 4th, 1860, the appointment was made in accordance with this request, and the first sermon preached by the pastor, under the separate organization, was on Sunday morning April 15th, from, "I am Sure that when I Come to You I shall Come in the Fullness of the Blessings of the Gospel of Christ."

The following members were transferred from Bethel in 1859, and formed the nucleus of St. Paul's, and the past and present prosperity of the latter is largely due to their earnest efforts and liberal contributions:

Mr. and Mrs. W. H. Rutan.
"   William Lamond.
"   Wm. H. Totten.
"   David Joline.
"   James Butler.
"   James W. Sprague.
"   John Lamond.
"   Aaron Van Name.
"   Abraham H. Wood.
"   Alexander Lamond.
"   E. Price Wood.
"   James M. Rutan.
"   Henry VanName.
"   Henry D. Romer.
"   Reuben Wood.
"   Horatio Arents.
"   Samuel Ward.
"   Kinzey Pepper.
"   John Skidmore.
"   David VanName.
"   Wm. Bloodgood.
"   Cornelius Palmer.
"   George Cole.
"   James W. Sleight.
"   John Christopher.
"   S. B. Sprague.
"   Abel Martin.
"   Adam C. Lyons.
"   J. W. Russell.

Mr. and Mrs. David DePew.
      "   Abraham Sprague, Jr.
      "   Cornelius Slaight.
      "   Wesley Patten.
      "   Edward Decker.
      "   Alfred Palmer.
      "   John Sharrott.
      "   George Dunville.
Dr. and Mrs. E. W. Hubbard.
Mrs. John I. Swaim.
    " Abraham Cole.
    " John Journeay.
    " C. C. Ellis.
    " Abigail LaForge.
    " Rachel Palmer.
    " Emily J. Wood (Mrs. W. T. Elliott).
Miss Emily Ward (Mrs. John White).
    " Letitia A. Falkenburg.
    " Mary E. Swaim.
    " Phebe Kinsey.
    " Letitia T. LaForge.
    " Margaret Lamond.
Mr. Abraham Sprague, Sr.
    " Henry Butler.
    " Joshua M. VanName.
    " J. P. Wortz.
    " William Reckhow.
    " Daniel Butler.
    " Apka B. Ward.
    " James L. Bedell.
    " Alvin A. Totten.

When St. Paul's congregation decided to organize a separate church, the members transferred from Bethel claimed that as they had helped to build

Bethel Church and parsonage, St. Paul's Church should receive a pro rata share of the value of the church property. The congregation and trustees of Bethel Church refused to admit this claim, and as the two congregations could not agree, the question was brought before the annual conference. That body decided that, according to the rule of the church in such cases, the church remained the sole property of the Bethel congregation, but that the parsonage property should be divided pro rata, according to the membership.

A meeting of all the trustees of both churches was, therefore, called, and held at Bethel parsonage on June 11th, 1860, to settle the amount which St. Paul's Church should receive for its share of the value of Bethel parsonage, based upon the membership of the two churches. The membership of Bethel, at that time, was found to be 203, and of St. Paul's, 126. After a full discussion of the matter, David Joline and Wm. H. Rutan, of St. Paul's, and E. J. Totten and M. S. Taylor, of Bethel, were appointed a committee to go over all matters in relation to the property and indebtedness, and to settle upon the amount due to St. Paul's Church. The final decision was that $665.02 was due St. Paul's Church, and upon the payment of this amount the trustees released all claim to Bethel property.

The first quarterly conference for St. Paul's Church was held at the parsonage June 30th, 1860. The presiding elder, the Rev. John S. Porter, decided that Abraham Sprague and James W. Sprague, having held the office of steward in Bethel Church, previous to their transfer to St. Paul's, should hold the office of steward in the new organization. The meeting then proceeded to elect the following, to make up the disciplinary number: James W. Slaight, S. B. Sprague, Daniel Butler, Henry Van-Name and Cornelius Slaight. Daniel Butler was elected recording steward, which office he has held continuously to the present time. The leaders present at this first conference were Wm. H. Rutan, James Butler, John S. Journeay, James M. Rutan and Henry D. Romer. Aaron Van Name, Wm. H. Rutan and James Butler were appointed a committee to estimate the amount necessary for the preacher's salary. Wm. H. Rutan was appointed a delegate to meet with the district stewards and estimate the amount necessary for the presiding elder's salary. James M. Rutan, David Joline and Henry D. Romer were appointed the missionary committees.

At the second quarterly conference, the preacher's salary was fixed at $600. The following year it was raised to $800.

St. Paul's Methodist Episcopal Church, of Totten-ville, was now fully organized. It had a pastor of its own, a full board of trustees and stewards, and a convenient but small house of worship.

The attendance increased rapidly under the able and eloquent preaching of the Rev. John S. Swaim, and the little church was soon crowded to its utmost capacity. The congregation soon saw that a larger building would be required, and began to agitate the question of building a church in front of the chapel, which, with commendable foresight, had been placed on the rear of the lot.

Mr. Swaim, having completed his three years, two at Bethel and one at St. Paul's, was succeeded in

1861, by the Rev. Charles Larew. In the early part
of Mr. Larew's ministry, the first steps were taken
toward building the new church. A meeting of the
congregation, called by the trustees, was held in
the chapel May 15th, 1861, and unanimously passed
a resolution authorizing the trustees to begin work
immediately. A committee was appointed. to for-
mulate plans.

At a meeting of the trustees held May 25th, the
pastor, the Rev. Charles Larew, reported that the
committee had selected as a model from which to
build the new church, one found in 37th street,
New York. The report was accepted, and a building committee appointed, consisting of Wm. H.
Rutan, James Butler, David Joline and Abraham
Sprague.

The trustees already had on the ground a large
quantity of brick left over from the building of the
chapel. They purchased the other material necessary and employed T. Kilpatrick, of New Jersey, to
put up the building. The new church was 45x60
feet with a seating capacity for over 400. Work
was begun in the summer of 1861, and the new
church was dedicated June 15th, 1862, by Bishop
Newman. The subscription on dedication day
amounted to $212.18.

During the autumn of 1861 and 1862 camp-meetings were held in the grove adjoining the church.
The trustees put up a large tent on the grounds
and the ladies of the congregation furnished re-
freshments for the many visitors, turning the
proceeds over to the building fund. By this means
$269.68 was added to the treasury in 1861, and
$404.40 in 1862, making a total $674.08.

The first organ was purchased in 1866, during the pastorate of the Rev. Thomas Walters. At a meeting of the trustees held August 1st of that year, David J. Pepper, Dr. Solomon Andrews and W. L. La Forge were appointed a committee to purchase a suitable organ and prepare a place for it. They selected a Mason & Hamlin organ, costing $750, and placed it in the gallery. This organ remained in use until 1890, when the present organ was procured. The bell, costing $275, was also purchased and hung the same year.

The question of building a parsonage had been discussed for some time, and in November 1866, the trustees purchased from Charles Drake the lot on which the parsonage now stands, for $700, giving their bond for the amount of the purchase price. Messrs. Henry Van Name and Wesley Wood, on behalf of the board of trustees, and Daniel Butler, on behalf of the congregation, were appointed a committee to select plans and erect the house. Work was begun at once and the parsonage, a very suitable and commodious building, was finished the next year, at a cost, as the treasurer's book shows, of $3,033.38. The work was done by Isaac S. Slaight and R. T. Hill, the trustees furnishing all the material.

In 1867, the annual conference was held in St. Paul's Church, Bishop Simpson, presiding. This was the first annual conference ever held in Tottenville.

Pews in St. Paul's Church were first rented in 1868, during the pastorate of the Rev. S. H. Opdyke. When the question was put to vote whether or not pews should be rented, at a meeting held May 3rd, the vote stood seventy in favor of and seven against.

The treasurer, in his report for 1869, gives the indebtedness of the church as $6,837, including mortgages of $5,000 on the church and parsonage, with a small cash balance on hand.

That year the pews rented for $1,334, and the pastor's salary was raised to $1,300. The following year the pew rent amounted to $1,536. This was during the pastorate of the Rev. Geo. F. Dickinson.

During the latter year, an effort was made to purchase land for cemetery purposes, and a committee was appointed to examine the property of Abraham Sprague, on Amboy road. The committee reported that the land was unsuitable for burying purposes, and the matter was dropped.

The next improvement to the church property was the purchase of a strip of land in the rear of the church, from Mr. Aspinwall. When Mr. Aspinwall was approached in the matter of selling the lot, 100x250 feet, he offered to submit the question of its value to two disinterested men, and to accept one-half the price at which it was appraised. The value was fixed in this manner at $2,000, and a contract made with Mr. Aspinwall for half that sum, but the transaction was not completed until 1874. Notwithstanding the improvements made to the property of the church, and the liberal salary paid to its pastor, its indebtedness had been considerably diminished, as the treasurer reports at that time that all debts had been paid, except two mortgages held by Jas. J. Winants, amounting together to $4,500. At the same time, the church and parsonage were valued at $15,000.

This debt remained on the church until 1881.

At a meeting of the trustees on Oct. 1st of that year, Mrs. Mary Wood came before the board of trustees and urged that a special and earnest effort be made to pay off the mortgage and free the church from debt. The suggestion was approved, and Sunday, the 13th of November, 1881, was set apart as the day when a determined effort should be made to raise the $4,500, and few who were present will ever forget the occasion. Mrs. Wood headed the subscription with $1,000, which she afterward increased to $1,100, and the others came forward and subscribed such sums as they felt able to give. When the amount was added up the total was found to amount to $3,550. This was soon afterward increased to $4,008, which with the $600 in the bank gave enough to pay off the entire mortgage and leave a small balance in the treasury. The $2,000 mortgage was paid on Nov. 6th, 1881, and the $2,500 mortgage on Jan. 30th, 1882, and the church saw itself free of bonded debt for the first time in over twenty years.

In 1883, David C. Butler, then superintendent of the Sunday-school, saw the necessity of having a larger room. Children were asking for admission to the school, who could not be accommodated. He went before the trustees of the church and asked permission to enlarge the room, offering to become responsible for all the expense. The question was brought before the congregation on February 13th, and Mr. Butler was given the privilege of making the desired alterations, by a vote of 59 to 1.

After appointing a committee, it was thought best to tear down the old chapel and erect an entirely new one, to be 75x50 feet, with infant department in the rear, to be closed up with sliding doors, both rooms to be seated with chairs to make it convenient for teaching.

Henry L. Sprague and James L. Bedell did the work. The whole cost of the building and furnishing was $3,800, which was all paid for in one year by hard work and perseverance on the part of the Sunday-school.

Two years after the building was erected it was beautifully painted and frescoed on the inside, at a cost of $250. The work was done by the late A. Thruelson. It was considered, at that time, by the presiding elder of the district, to be the most beautiful and most convenient Sunday-school room in the Newark conference. The ventilation was through the ceiling, which was 20 feet high.

One of the attractions of the room was the stationary blackboards in front of the room, for instruction and explanation of the lessons. The beautiful illustrations drawn by the artist, D. J. Pepper, were much admired and were highly instructive and interesting.

The seating capacity of the room was 450. At the time of the erection, and for several years afterward, the number of scholars was 450, and one of the principal features of the school room was the large number of adults that attended the school.

In 1886, the Ladies' Aid Society was organized to raise money to pay off the outstanding indebtedness. This society has proved one of the most successful financial aids to the church, and in the last few years has raised large sums of money.

In the following year, it was decided to have the church decorated and frescoed inside and to purchase new lamps and make other needed improvements. Messrs. J. S. Sleight, Paul Van Name, H. L. Sprague, James W. Sprague and Henry D. Romer were appointed a committee to confer with the Ladies' Aid Society in regard to raising funds for these improvements. This work was done in 1887, by the late A. Thruelson.

The Ladies' Aid Society concluded to continue their work and to raise money to replace the old, unsightly board walk with concrete. Having raised sufficient money, a contract was made the next year with Messrs. Wolff & Son, of Stapleton, who put down the present massive and substantial walks, at a cost of $400.

The next important improvement was made in 1890. The church, having received a legacy of $1,953.55 from the estate of the late O. A. Wood, and $1,000 from the estate of Mrs. Mary Wood, the congregation voted to use this money for the purchase of a new pipe organ and for a new roof and other improvements to the building. A new organ was therefore purchased from Messrs. Jardine & Sons, of New York, costing $2,200, and about $300 was ⋅ expended in enlarging the pulpit platform for the organ and building a suitable place for the choir, and $700 for a new slate roof, the contract for the latter being awarded to Wm. H. Daggett.

The old stoves were removed in 1895, and a contract made with John B. Wood to put in the J. L. Mott system of steam heaters. The work was finished that fall.

The people of St. Paul's can look back to many years of hard work and much self-denial to secure a suitable place of worship, but they must feel that

WILLIAM LAMOND,
First Superintendent of St. Paul's Sunday School, and
Teacher for over thirty years.

in their present fine and commodious church and Sunday-school rooms, they are reaping rich compensation for their labor.

ST. PAUL'S PASTORS.

1859-6c—John S. Swaim, died at Jacksonville, Fla., Nov. 18th, 1875, aged 69 years; 41 years in ministry.

1861-2—Charles Larew, supernumerary, residence at Mendham, N. J.; entered ministry in 1847.

1863—James Ayars, died at New Providence, N. J., Jan. 23rd, 1880, aged 75 years; 51 years in ministry.

1864-6—Thomas Walters, died at Hackensack, N. J., July 7th, 1879, aged 55 years; 30 years in ministry.

1867-8—S. H. Opdyke, died at Newton, N. J., Oct. 21st, 1880, aged 53 years; 23 years in ministry.

1869-71—George F. Dickinson, stationed at Allendale, N. J.; entered ministry in 1854.

1872-3—David Walters, supernumerary, residence at Lebanon, N. J.; entered ministry in 1852.

1874-6—Jacob P. Dailey, died at Bethlehem, Pa., April 10th, 1883, aged 63 years; 38 years in ministry.

1877-9—J. B. Taylor, stationed at Montville, N. J; entered ministry in 1865.

1880-1—Solomon Parsons, died at Paterson, N. J., in 1897; 39 years in ministry.

1882-4—William H. Ruth, stationed at Westfield, N. J.; entered ministry in 1872.

1885-7—Thomas E. Gordon, stationed at Harrison, N. J.; entered the ministry in 1859.

1888-90—J. R. Bryan, D. D., stationed at Mariners' Harbor, N. Y.; entered ministry in 1848.

1891-3—C. F. Hull, stationed at Jersey City, N. J.;
entered ministry in 1877.

1894-6—W. S. McCowan, D. D., stationed at Jersey
City, N. J.; entered ministry in 1869.

1897—R. B. Collins, present pastor; entered ministry 1863.

PRESENT OFFICIALS.

TRUSTEES:

Daniel Skidmore, president; Geo. H. Hart, secre-
tary; H. L. Sprague, treasurer; E. P. Manee, P. M.
Van Name, T. P. Rutan, Taylor Clayton, John N.
White, Calvin Vidian.

STEWARDS:

Daniel Butler, recording secretary; Henry Romer,
Job Derickson, Almer Decker, J. M. Rutan, Richard
Christopher, Geo. Leavitt, Theodore Leven, Geo.
Rolle, David Coleman, M. D.

Chorister, John N. White.

Organist, Miss Grace Ellis.

EPWORTH LEAGUE:

The Simpson Epworth League No. 6036, of St.
Paul's M. E. Church, was formed at a meeting held
June 9th, 1891, with thirty-nine charter members,
and the following officers were elected:

R. O. Sprague, president; D. C. Butler, first vice-
president; Richard Christopher, second vice-president; Chas. U. Thrall, third vice-president; John N.
White, fourth vice-president; W. B. Butler, secretary; C. T. VanDeusen, financial secretary.

At the next meeting held one week later, forty-
two new members were added to the roll.

The present membership is 143, with the following officers:

Geo. P. Sullivan, president; Geo. H. Hart, first

vice-president; Mrs. W. H. Felch, second vice-president; Miss Jessie Crellin, third vice-president; Miss Grace Peterson, fourth vice-president; W. E. Smith, corresponding secretary; Mrs. R. O. Sprague, treasurer.

JUNIOR EPWORTH LEAGUE:

Samuel Cunningham, president; Miss Myra Rolle, vice-president; Miss Ada Ainsworth, secretary; Samuel Hopping, treasurer; Miss Hessie Pendexter, chairman entertainment committee; Miss Violet Hopping, chairman mercy and help department; Miss Florence Cole, chairman literary department; Miss Marjorie Barnes, pianist; Powell Cronk, chorister; Mrs. R. W. Wood and Mrs. J. L. Dailey, superintendents.

LADIES' BIBLE CIRCLE:

Mrs. George E. Rolle, president; Mrs. J. L. Dailey, secretary; Mrs. Wm. Felch, treasurer.

LADIES' AID:

Mrs. Henry Rutan, president; Mrs. Daniel Skidmore, vice-president; Mrs. C. T. Van Deusen, secretary; Mrs. R. O. Wood, treasurer.

AUXILIARY OF WOMAN'S FOREIGN MISSIONARY SOCIETY:

Mrs. R. W. Wood, president; Mrs. Caroline Sleight, Mrs. Theodore Leven, Mrs. E. P. Manee, Mrs. Jennie Henderson, vice-presidents; Mrs. William Felch, recording secretary; Mrs. George W. Sprague, corresponding secretary; Mrs. John L. Dailey, treasurer.

SUNDAY-SCHOOL:

The Sunday-school was organized as soon as the chapel was opened for service, and William Lamond was elected the first superintendent, and served until he resigned to join the army during the Civil war.

The first musical instrument used in St. Paul's Church was the organ bought by the Sunday-school, from a Christmas offering made at the earnest solicitation of James M. Rutan, while he was superintendent.

David C. Butler has served the longest term, having been superintendent twenty-two years. Since its organization the school has had thirteen superintendents, as follows:

Wm. Lamond, Horatio Arents, Edward Decker, James M. Rutan, Wm. LaForge, David C. Butler, Paul M. VanName, David C. Butler, J. C. Windsor, David C. Butler, D. B. Skidmore, Geo. H. Hart, and the present superintendent.

The present officers are:

R. O. Sprague, superintendent; Geo. H. Hart, treasurer; W. E. Smith, secretary; Geo. P. Sullivan, assistant secretary; Geo. W. Slaight, librarian; C. T. VanDeusen, Arthur H. White, Robert D. Powers, assistant librarians; Miss Lizzie Sprague, Miss Bertha Collins, Miss Fannie_Haines, Miss Florence Dailey, pianists.

PRESENT MEMBERSHIP.

Mr. and Mrs. Daniel Butler.
"   "   William Lamond.
"   "   George Leavitt.
"   "   Alfred Palmer.
"   "   Wesley Patten.
"   "   Melancthon Rutan.
"   "   Henry Rutan.
"   "   J. W. Russell.
"   "   Henry D. Romer.

D. C. BUTLER.
Superintendent of St. Paul's Sunday School
twenty-two years.

Mr. and Mrs. A. E. Rolle.
    "   Henry L. Sprague.
    "   John M. Sleight.
    "   Reuben O. Sprague.
    "   Isaac Slaight.
    "   D. B. Skidmore.
    "   George W. Slaight.
    "   William H. Totten.
    "   Paul M. Van Name.
    "   Charles T. Van Deusen.
    "   Reuben O. Wood.
    "   John N. White.
    "   Calvin Vidian.
    "   Joseph C. Windsor.
    "   George H. Sleight.
    "   David C. Butler.
    "   James L. Bedell.
    "   Jacob W. Cole.
    "   Richard Christopher.
Dr. and Mrs. David Coleman.
Mr. and Mrs. Taylor Clayton.
    "   Palmer W. Copeland.
    "   Job Derickson.
    "   John L. Dailey.
    "   Edward Derickson.
    "   Almer Decker.
    "   Walter T. Elliott.
    "   W. H. Felch.
    "   George H. Hart.
    "   D. A. Joline.
    "   Louis F. Johnson.
    "   Theodore Leven.
    "   Moses A. Letts.
    "   Abel Martin.

Mr. and Mrs. Alfred Moore.
      "   D. J. Pepper.
      "   John C. Murphy.
      "   Freeman Palmer.
      "   John Paugh.
      "   George Russell.
      "   George E. Rolle.
      "   George W. Sprague.
      "   William B. Skidmore.
      "   Frank Skidmore.
      "   Edward Sleight.
      "   John B. Wood.
      "   Irving Sleight.
      "   Melville Decker.
Mrs. John Journeay.
   "   John D. Manee.
   "   Isaac Moore.
   "   William Palmer.
   "   George Penhallow.
   "   William Pepper.
   "   Rufus Paugh.
   "   Charles Thrall.
   "   Charles Williams.
   "   W. H. Smith.
   "   Eber Butler.
   "   William Bedell.
   "   Myron Brown.
   "   John Brown.
   "   John Cole.
   "   Enoch Corson.
   "   John White.
   "   Harry Clover.
   "   George Cunningham.
   "   Gabriel Dissosway.

Mrs. William Derickson.
" R. B. Collins.
" Raymond Ellis.
" George C. Hubbard.
" Fred Hopping.
" John Hopping.
" Frances Everett.
" Ella F. Ford.
" Harriet Graham.
" Emma T. Hudson.
" Martha Irving.
" Ellen Joline.
" Marilda LaForge.
" Priscilla Decker.
" Kate E. Davis.
" Martha A. Pepper.
" Esther Wood.
" Celia Ellis.
" Catherine Christopher.
" Elizabeth Clark.
" Margaret A. Decker.
" Caroline Burgess.
" Eliza Cole.
" Sarah A. Woglom.
" Lina Dorsey.
" Helen J. VanMeerbeke.
" Helen L. Ward.
" Ida Wood.
" Elizabeth Smith.
" Sarah Van Name.
" Ella A. NanName.
" Cordelia W. Reckhow.
" Phebe J. Sprague.
" Caroline Sleight.

Miss Grace E. Peterson.
    "   Mary E. Pearsall.
    "   Gilbertine Sleight.
    "   Anna C. VanName.
    "   Della VanName.
    "   Kate L. Wood.
    "   Leone B. Williams.
    "   Jennie B. Wood.
    "   Eva Skidmore.
    "   Annie Sullivan.
    "   Ida Bedell.
    "   Annie E. Cole.
    "   Julia Cole.
    "   Bertha Collins.
    "   Bessie Coleman.
    "   Mary C. Corson.
    "   Mamie Derickson.
    "   Josephine E. Joline.
    "   Grace Johnson.
    "   Fannie Joline.
    "   Fannie Lucas.
    "   Kate L. Leven.
    "   Kate C. Hubbard.
    "   Fannie Haines.
    "   Belle Haines.
    "   Willabelle Irving.
    "   Phebe E. Noon.
Mr. E. Stewart Manee.
Dr. H. V. McCormick.
Mr. George E. W. Oakley.
  "   DeWitt Pepper.
  "   George Pepper.
  "   Peter Johnson.
  "   John H. Leven.

Mrs. Mary W. Pendexter.

Mr. E. P. Manee.

" George Dunville.

" Arthur White.

" Samuel Cunningham.

" William B. Butler.

" Frank E. Sullivan.

" John D. Sharrott.

" William E. Smith.

" Warren M. Van Name.

" John Skidmore.

" Charles C. Thrall.

" Alvin A. Totten.

" George P. Sullivan.

" Harry D Romer.

" James M. Sprague.

" Cornelius Sleight.

" Robert A. Powers.

" George W. Pendexter.

" James M. Rutan.

" Theodore P. Rutan.

Dr. R. H. Duncan:

ST. MARK'S M. E. CHURCH,

PLEASANT PLAINS, NEW YORK.

ST. MARK'S M. E. CHURCH.
Pleasant Plains.

CHAPTER VI.

_____

_____

THE foundations of the society now known as St. Mark's Methodist Episcopal Church of Prince Bay, were laid as early as the year 1837, when under the pastorate of the Rev. Mulford Day, a gracious revival was held in Bethel Church, which then constituted a part of the old Woodrow charge. As a result of this revival Pastor Day found it advisable to organize a class in this district, which, up to that date, was practically unoccupied. Thomas Butler was selected as leader and for a number of years conducted the class which was regularly held at the house of Nicholas La Forge, an old residence then occupying the site where Benz's saloon is now situated.

In 1841, another revival of large influence and power was held in Woodrow (the mother church), under the pastorate of the Rev. Wesley Robertson. As a result of this revival another class was formed in the upper part of the village for the especial benefit of those new converts and members connected with Woodrow congregation. William Manee was assigned to this class, which met in the the old homestead of Joseph Bedell, who continued its leadership until the separation of Bethel and Woodrow charges in 1842.

Israel La Forge was then appointed his successor and continued in charge of the class work for many years. In the early fifties the class under the leadership of Thomas Butler was merged into this class, thereby practically uniting the district and preparing the way for opening a preaching servce in the old school-house in 1854, under the pastorate of the Rev. Benjamin Kelly. These services were regularly maintained under the various pastors of Woodrow until the year 1871. A Sunday-school was also organized about that time, which has continued to be a most valuable auxiliary to the church up to the present time.

During the ministry of Abram M Palmer in 1861, a desire was substantially manifested by the worshipers in the old school-house to possess a more commodious and comfortable place of worship. A fund for this purpose was raised by means of festivals, etc., and when $1,000 had been secured, the site on which the present church edifice and parsonage are located, was bought, and through the generosity of John Latourette, who donated the sum of $200, the society was enabled to secure the grounds free of debt.

Several years elapsed before the congregation erected the church edifice, but each successive pastorate brought them nearer to the realization of their cherished hopes, and in 1871, under the pastorate of the Rev. Jeremiah Cowins, the church was built at a cost of $7,500, of which $4,500 was provided for on the day of dedication. The remaining $3,000

was secured on bond and mortgage at seven per
cent., from Mrs. Elsie Latourette.

Soon after the erection of the building it was
discovered that the building committee had made a
serious mistake in substituting a slate for a shingle
roof, as the frame work was only intended to support the latter. As a result, the congregation was at
once put to an additional expense of several hundred dollars in making the structure secure.

In 1873, the charge began its independent life,
the congregation having overruled the decision of
the quarterly conference to remain united with
Woodrow charge, and the Rev. A. Van Deusen was
appointed its first pastor. This appointment made
necessary the provision of a parsonage. The
enterprise was at once undertaken and a comfortable house was provided for the pastor at a cost of
$2,000, one-half of which was immediately secured.

Mr. Van Deusen's pastorate was marked by the
development of the spiritual and temporal interests
of the church, and extended from March 1873 to
March 1876. During the fall of 1876, in the first
year of the pastorate of the Rev. W. C. Nelson, a mission was opened and maintained for a considerable
time at Giffords station, Dr. S. M. Vail, a retired
minister and a member of St Mark's quarterly conference, took charge of this work. A Sunday-school
was organized, and preaching services were held
every Sunday evening. George Colon donated a plot
of ground for the erection of a chapel, a board of
trustees was elected and a few hundred dollars
were raised toward the building; but for some reason the enterprise failed, and the Moravian brethren have now succeeded where the Methodists

failed. Mr. Nelson's pastorate lasted two years and he was succeeded by the Rev. J. E. Hancock whose pastorate continued for three years, from 1878 to 1881. Mr. Hancock succeeded in liquidating the debt of $1,000 on the parsonage and advancing the benevolent offerings of the church.

In the spring of 1881, the Rev. J. R. Daniels succeeded Mr. Hancock and served as pastor for two years. During this period the church had a very unusual experience. This was a midsummer revival, the result of which remains to this day and ought always be a standing rebuke to those Christians who confine the operations of God's saving power to one season of the year.

Two special events characterized the pastorate of the Rev. Geo. W. Miller which began in March 1883 and ended March 1885. The first was the payment of $520 on the church debt and a reduction of the interest on the remaining indebtedness from seven per cent. to six per cent. This was the first effort in this direction since the dedication of the church.

The second was the re-ceiling of the church with white pine, frescoing the walls, re-furnishing the pulpit and the purchase of new lamps for the church, all at a cost of $900.

In 1885, the Rev. I. N. Vansant was appointed pastor and filled a term of three years. This period marks a great revival of the benevolent and spiritual interest of the church. Extra meetings were commenced in January 1886. For a month there seemed to be no indication of a revival, still the effort was continued; and at length the work opened with great power, such as many had never witnessed before: the entire community was stirred. The meetings continued up to the time of conference and about eighty persons were received on probation. At the conclusion of the probationary period sixty-eight probationers were received into full membership at one time. This was the most inspiring scene ever witnessed in St Mark's Church. Subsequently three others were received, making a total of seventy-one. The Sunday-school was greatly benefited by the revival. Winant Androvette was the superintendent and the school was very prosperous under his administration.

During this year the church was repainted, the windows were altered; the granolithic walk was laid, the fence was repaired and made lower and a coal and wood house built, all at a cost of $500. These improvements added much to the beauty and comfort of the church.

In the year of 1887, the revival resulted in seven conversions, five of whom were finally received into full membership.

On July 26th of that year, during a most terrific thunder storm, the church was struck by lightning, shattering the belfry, tearing off weather boards and wainscoting in the vestibule, damaging the roof and breaking the wall in the rear of the pulpit. All damage was covered by insurance, which amounted to $200. The church was struck just before the hour of service and when the bell sounded the alarm many thought it was the usual service bell. They were not long, however, in discovering their mistake, and the true facts of the case, and many hastened with buckets to avoid a catastrophe by fire. The pastor and his family received a shock, from which they were some time in recovering. All felt grateful to God that the church was saved from conflagration, that no lives were lost and comparatively little damage was done. This year C. A. Shea was re-elected superintendent of the Sunday-school, and its prosperity continued.

The closing year of this pastorate was not marked by any revival spirit. There were no conversions, yet the attendance upon the means of grace was a source of gratification and the benevolence this year reached the roll of honor.

Only one thing was needed to make this period a monumental epoch in the history of the church, and that was, systematic organization; zeal without a means of assimilation prevents perpetuity. Therefore, this period was followed by an unavoidable decline in the benevolent and spiritual life of the church.

The Rev. E. V. King succeeded to the next pastoral term which lasted four years, from April 1888 to April 1892. During this period, nineteen persons were received on probation and six by letter, or on profession of faith.

The old indebtedness of the church was entirely canceled by legacies.

The kitchen of the parsonage was improved, new furniture and carpet were provided for the parlor, and other comforts added to the pastor's residence. During the last year of this term extensive improvements were made upon the church edifice. In August 1891, the church was closed for that purpose and was not reopened until December 6th.

The church edifice was moved about thirty feet further from the street, a neatly finished and fur-

nished lecture-room was built underneath, the walls
of the auditorium were repapered, a new pulpit and
choir platform was erected, an attractive vestibule
superseded the old one, and a neat little kitchen
was built at the rear of the church, all at a cost of
$4,500, $2,000 of which was provided for on the day
of reopening. About this time Mr. King organized
" The Ladies' Aid," a society which since has been of
inestimable value to all the financial interests of the
church. The temporal prosperity of this period has
but one thing to mar it, the decline of the spiritual
and benevolent interests of the society. The class-
meetings ceased to exist and the prayer-meetings
were poorly attended.

In April 1892, the great itinerant wheel of the
church once more revolved and the Rev. James Clayton Howard was appointed pastor by Bishop Thomas
Bowman, the senior bishop of the church. This
pastorate covered the full term of five years and
marks a period of organization with normal, temporal,
spiritual, benevolent, intellectual and social development.

During the first year, 1892-1893, the class-meetings
were re-established and organized, the Epworth
League, which has since made such a noble record,
was organized, all the benevolences were advanced,
a floating debt of about $500 was paid, and the par-
sonage was enlarged and internally remodeled and
refurnished at a cost of more than $600, without
incurring debt.

The year closed with a glorious revival resulting
in more than sixty conversions, fifty-seven of whom
were admitted on probation and six by letter or on
profession of faith.

The second year, 1893-1894, was marked by the organization of "the department of mercy and help," a department of the Epworth League, which has made many hearts light and is doing most practical Christian work. This year a "birthday fund" was also established in behalf of the Sunday-school library, with good results. Both the senior and junior Cadet Corps were organized for the moral and social uplifting of the boys and young men. $500 was paid on the church debt and incidental improvements to church grounds and property were made. Fourteen were received on probation and forty-nine from probation into full membership. The social means of grace were well established and the general benevolence again increased.

In the third year, 1894-1895, twelve were received from probation into full membership and one by letter. The financial system of the trustees was reorganized to the great advantage of the church, $500 more was paid on the church debt, the church and parsonage were repainted, the foundation of the church coated with cement, the chimneys repaired and a new well dug, furnishing water in both the church kitchen and the parsonage. The Ladies' Aid improved the pulpit and choir platform and altar with new curtains and stained all the wood-work; they also repapered the parsonage parlor and stained the wood-work, all costing about $300, and all paid for.

This year the congregation extended their hospitality in cordial welcome and entertainment to a part of the annual conference which held its business sessions in Bethel Church and its anniversaries in St. Paul's, Bethel and St. Mark's.

The fourth year, 1895-1896, places St. Mark's Church high on the roll of honor in her benevolences, standing fourth out of fifty-five churches in the district. This year another revival was experienced with some unusual manifestations of spiritual power. At a morning service, after the conclusion of the sermon, and in the midst of the closing prayer, a burdened soul was heard to weep and call upon God for help. She was a lady much beloved by all, yet she was without the witness of God's saving power. As the closing hymn was sung she advanced to the altar asking God to help her. The congregation wept and prayed and sang and soon the praises of a new-born soul filled the house of God with glory. Such a Sunday morning service is seldom seen.

Another marked instance was the struggle of a discouraged soul reaching the point of utter despair and desperation. Her physical powers were entirely exhausted and some thought she was dying. But the pastor reassured each who became unduly alarmed, and in a few moments God in his own way had changed despair into hope, spiritual death into spiritual life. Another was added to the great throng who appreciate the blessed truth that "God so loved the world that He gave his only begotten Son, that whosoever believeth on Him should not perish but have everlasting life." Twenty-two were received on probation as a result of this work of grace, and six by letter.

This year a thorough revision of the record of church membership was made and about thirty - five who had ceased to make any profession of religion or had removed and made no communication, were crossed from the roll. Many had been lost sight of for years.

The fifth year, 1896-1897, is but half completed and the historian finds his data meagre. Twenty-two probationers were received into full membership. The literary department in the early part of this year, was thoroughly reorganized with a most efficient and successful leader, R. G. Gandy, in connection with which a sprightly and up-to-date church journal was published.

This year the Ladies' Aid renovated the parsonage kitchen and dining-room, repairing the walls, and repapering and repainting both rooms. They recarpeted the parlor and hall stairs and provided a couch for the dining-room. The trustees laid a thorough system of terra-cotta drainage around the building and grounds. All these improvements were also made without incurring debt. It is a great source of satisfaction to both pastor and people to know that within the short period of five years the church has increased her offerings to all interests sixty-five per cent. In view of the fact that many secular interests have made large demands upon the resources of the community within that time, these results are all the more gratifying and show that the energy and life of the church may be depended upon for still greater work for good.

——— o ———

In 1897, the Rev. W. E. Blakeslee was appointed to St. Mark's. His pastorate has been successful, although not many names have been added to the roll of membership. All assessments have been fully paid, services are well attended and church and Sunday-school are in a healthful condition.

JAMES LEWIS.
Member of Official Board for over twenty years.

ST. MARK'S PASTORS.

1873-5—Albert VanDeusen, stationed at Bayonne, N. J.; entered ministry in 1866.

1876-7—Wm. C. Nelson, stationed at East Millstone, N. J.; entered ministry in 1853.

1878-81—J. E. Hancock, stationed at Succasunna, N. J.; entered ministry in 1865.

1881-2—J. R. Daniels, stationed at Ocean Grove, N. J.; entered ministry in 1860.

1883-5—Geo. W. Miller, died at Little Falls, N. J., Nov 15th, 1896, aged 56 years; 27 years in ministry.

1885-7—I. N. Vansant, died at Stony Point, N. Y. aged 67 years; 38 years in ministry.

1888-92—E. V. King, stationed at Phillipsburg, N. J., entered ministry in 1866.

1892-6—J. C. Howard, stationed at Stapleton, N. Y.; entered ministry in 1887.

1897—W. E. Blakeslee, present pastor; entered ministry in 1858.

The members transferred from Woodrow in 1873 are the following:

Mr. and Mrs. C. C. Androvette.
       "   James Androvette.
       "   Winant S. Androvette.
       "   John Androvette.
       "   Alfred Bedell.
       "   Eugene B. Halle.
       "   Sebastian LaForge.
       "   William H. Sharrott.

Mrs. Mary M. Johnson.
   "   Emeline W. Manee.
   "   Elsie Latourette.
Mr. Israel LaForge.
   "   Jacob W. Sleight.

Robert Lyons, superintendent; D. O. DePew, assistant superintendent; Mrs. A. W. Browne, second assistant superintendent; Chester Brown, secretary; Edwin Shea, assistant secretary; Mrs. A. W. Decker, treasurer; Alfred Cawse and William Swade, librarians;Miss Edith Sprague, organist.

EPWORTH LEAGUE:

The Epworth League was organized during the pastorate of the Rev. E. V. King. Geo. D. Heck was chosen the first president and has served continuously up to the present time.

George Heck, president; Joseph Simonson, first vice-president; Mrs. R. G. Gandy, second vice-president; Miss Maude Cawse, fourth vice-president; Mrs. A. W. Browne, secretary; Mrs. George D. Heck, treasurer; Miss E. Pounding, chairman lookout committee.

LIST OF PRESENT MEMBERS.

Mr. and Mrs. C. C. Androvette.
" 	 James A. Androvette.
" 	 Winant S. Androvette.
" 	 Elmer Bedell.
" 	 John Androvette.
" 	 Arthur Browne.
" 	 Joseph T. Androvette.
" 	 George T. Androvette.
" 	 William Burke.
" 	 Albert A. Bryan.
" 	 Cornelius DePew.
" 	 Irving W. Decker.
" 	 William G. Davison.
" 	 David O. DePew.
" 	 Samuel Eddy.
" 	 Joseph A. Forester.

Mr. and Mrs. James Graham.
    "   R. G. Gandy.
    "   George D. Heck.
    "   Nelson Jacklin.
    "   Thomas Jobes.
    "   David Johnson.
    "   Joseph B. Lewis.
    "   Francis A. Leggett.
    "   Nicholas LaForge.
    "   John F. Lewis.
    "   Albert LaForge.
    "   Robert K. Lyons.
    "   William W. Manee.
    "   William T. Manee.
    "   John Mersereau.
    "   Henry S. Marshall.
    "   George A. Marshall.
    "   A. J. Pasco.
    "   C. A. Shea.
    "   John W. Sprague.
    "   Stephen Swade.
    "   James H. Seaman.
    "   Charles B. Sprague.
    "   Reuben Simonson.
    "   Joseph H. Simonson.
    "   Minard Sharrott.
    "   Wesley Thompson.
    "   Henry S. VanWagner.
    "   Jesse G. Winant.
Dr. and Mrs. A. D. Decker.
Mrs. C. C. Bedell.
   " James Freude.
   " Henry Chapin.
   " George E. Cole.

Mrs. George Doty.
   "   Edward Ellis.
   "   Frank Goodwin.
   "   Henry Latourette.
   "   James Latourette.
   "   George White.
   "   John Marshall.
   "   Adelbert Price.
   "   Abram J. Sharrott.
   "   George Sprague.
   "   Leland K. Tarbox.
   "   D. W. Winant.
   "   Jane R. Marshall.
   "   Sarah M. Manee.
   "   Florence Oppermann.
   "   Mary J. Sharrott.
   "   Jane Sprague.
   "   Mary A. Sprague.
   "   Susan Totten.
   "   Sarah R. Van Allen.
   "   Matilda Wood.
   "   Sarah K. Weir.
   "   Sarah Wood.
   "   Rachel A. Townsend.
   "   Elizabeth Wood.
   "   Catherine Wood.
   "   Armenia Bedell.
   "   Hannah Butler.
   "   Emma J. Cawse.
   "   Elizabeth Eddy.
   "   Eva Halle.
   "   Catherine M. Hoag.
   "   Mary M. Johnson.
   "   Mary Jobes.

Mrs. Elizabeth Kirby.
   " Elsie Latourette.
   " Emily J. LaForge.
   " Henrietta LaForge.
Miss Mary L. Androvette.
   " Emeline Androvette.
   " Abbie S. Bedell.
   " Adeline Bedell.
   " Fanny R. Bedell.
   " Charlotte E. Bedell.
   " Maud Cawse.
   " Florence Cawse.
   " Hattie L. Davison.
   " Florence A. Decker.
   " Lucy M. Bedell.
   " Lulu Doty.
   " Neil Doty.
   " Adelia Grant.
   " Sadie Goodwin.
   " Sarah C. Halle.
   " Emeline C. Bedell.
   " Bessie Bedell.
   " Fannie Bedell.
   " Edith M. Wood.
   " Mary Jobes.
   " Nellie Leggett.
   " Mina La Forge.
   " Gertrude Manee.
   " Emma Manee.
   " Anna Polhemus.
   " Mary L. Oppermann.
   " Jennie Manee.
   " Maud Manee.
   " Eleanor C. Seaman.

Miss. Mabel Manee.
    "   Anna B. Manee.
    "   Maggie Weir.
    "   Bessie Manee.
    "   Edith Manee.
    "   Sarah Van Allen.
Mr. William F. Bedell.
    "   Alonzo Bedell.
    "   Charles H. Brown.
    "   George Ellis.
    "   James Lewis.
    "   William W. Lewis.
    "   William W. La Forge.
    "   James F. Purdy.
    "   George Pearsall.
    "   Jacob W. Sleight.
    "   Harry Sharrott.|
    "   Wilbur E. Shea.
    "   Edwin Shea.
    "   Charles Wood.

ST. JOHN'S M. E. CHURCH,

ROSSVILLE, NEW YORK.

CHAPTER VII.

ST. JOHN's M. E. CHURCH, of Rossville, was first established as a mission, or chapel, for the convenience of those members of the church and congregation who lived at Rossville and vicinity.

As early as 1854, it was thought best to erect a separate house of worship, the services to be under the charge of the pastor at Woodrow, and leaders appointed for that purpose. A lot was purchased in September of that year, for $325. This site was near the spot where the first Methodist sermons were preached on Staten Island, in the house of the late Peter Van Pelt, by Francis Asbury.

Work was begun on the new building in November 1854, and the church was dedicated on May 2nd, 1855.

The building was used for class and prayer meetings, Sunday-school and day school. In September 1856, preaching services were held Sunday afternoons, which were continued until November 1857, when preaching was held afternoon and evening. This was objected to by a number of the Woodrow members, and the evening service was discontinued in April 1858, and only afternoon meetings were held from that time until November 1860, when afternoon and evening meetings were resumed and continued until March 1861.

The mother church again objecting, the evening meetings were the second time omitted, and only one service was held each Sunday until January 1863. From that date, only occasional services were held in the evening, but the afternoon service was regularly kept up until April 1875, when evening service became quite regular, and as the Rossville members of the mother church were paying the larger portion of the preacher's salary, and bearing more than two-thirds of the church expenses, and as the spiritual interest of the Woodrow charge was to a very large extent centered in Rossville, the preacher in charge, the Rev. Milton Relyea, determined that Sunday evening services must be held regularly in Rossville. These continued during the year, and in that year and the beginning of 1876, a glorious revival broke out which resulted in the conversion of thirty-five in the village of Rossville.

By a special act of the legislature, in 1865, the chapel was incorporated as a separate church organization, and the society was formed under the name of "St. John's M. E. chapel."

At a duly advertised meeting to choose trustees, held May 13th, 1865, the following were elected: John Cole, three years; James J. Winants, three years; Cornelius Winant, two years; Jacob Winant, two years; Samuel W. Benedict, one year; Peter L. Cortelyou, one year.

John Cole was elected president of the board of trustees, Jacob Winant, secretary, and Peter L. Cortelyou, treasurer.

In the winter of 1867, the Rev. Geo. W. Treat, pastor, a subscription was raised to pay off the debt of the church, and $830.50 was subscribed.

In 1874, the chapel was painted and furnished at a cost of $215.77, the walks were flagged and other improvements made, costing $184.13.

In 1876, St. John's was set apart as a separate charge by the annual conference and the Rev. Salmon D. Jones was appointed first pastor. This action was taken by the conference on account of the dissatisfaction expressed by the members of Woodrow congregation, who objected to being limited to one service on Sunday. It may be doubted whether or not this was a wise step, for either parish, for fifteen years later, the Rev. Nicholas Vansant, who was then pastor, in his first quarterly report, says:

"Fifteen years ago (1876), St. John's Church was organized with 102 members and 28 probationers, in all, 130. Through death, removals and withdrawals, that number has been reduced to 50, and it is easy to foresee that unless relief comes, in some Providential way, and especially in a thorough revival of spirituality, unity and zeal, this church, in the near future, must resume its original place as a part of the Woodrow charge."

Mr. Jones remained three years, and, during his pastoral term, the chapel was enlarged at a cost of nearly $1,000, and greatly improved, and the church seemed to be, in every way, prosperous.

In August 1879, when the property opposite the church, now known as Orlando hall, was sold at public auction, it was bought by Messrs. Jesse Oakley and John Cole, as a committee in behalf of the trustees of the church, for $400. The trustees were thereupon authorized to borrow $700 to pay for the property, and to make such alterations as should render it suitable for the holding of entertainments, festivals and meetings other than church services. The present horse sheds were erected at that time.

The Ladies' Aid Society was formed in 1882, by Mrs. Sidell, Mrs. Miller and Mrs. John Burgher. This society, during the past fifteen years, has done much efficient work and has been one of the most important factors in raising money in support of the services and improvement of the church property.

The pews were first rented during the early part of the Rev. J. A. Kingsbury's pastorate. At a meeting held April 29th, 1884, to decide whether or not the pews should be rented, the vote stood 27 to 3 in favor of the measure. Prices were put upon the different pews, ranging from $12.50 to $5, the total rental value amounting to $400, ten pews being left free.

At the next quarterly meeting, Mr. Kingsbury reported that nearly all of the pews had been rented and the system gave promise of working satisfactorily. Three years later, however, the renting of pews was abandoned and the old system of subscriptions was revived.

During the autumn of this year, extensive repairs were made on the church, the foundations were rebuilt, the grounds graded, and the walls and ceiling papered and frescoed and the woodwork grained and painted. New lamps were purchased, new carpets, stoves, etc. The improvements made this

THE LATE REV. JESSE OAKLEY.

year cost $420, which was paid by subscriptions and the receipts of the harvest festival.

In 1890, the church received the legacy of the late O. A. Wood, amounting to $1,946.84. A portion of this money was used to pay off the outstanding indebtedness on the church, and a portion for rebuilding the hall, which, in honor of Mr. Wood, was named Orlando hall.

The following year, a deed of the parsonage was presented to the church by Mrs. Mary J. Winants, in accordance with the will of her husband, the late James Johnson Winants.

During the past two years, St. John's has had no resident pastor. The pulpit has been supplied by the Rev. A. A. Anderson, who visited Rossville each week, remaining over Sunday and conducting the services.

Our readers must not suppose that the fact that St. John's Church has not been so prosperous as many of the other Methodist Episcopal churches on Staten Island, is in any degree owing to the want of zeal or liberality on the part of either the membership or congregation.

Rossville lies off the line of rapid communication with the city, and on this account, while other portions of the Island have made rapid growth, Rossville has been almost at a standstill, and therefore there have been no new residents to take the place of the old members who have been removed by death.

And in this respect St. John's has been especially afflicted, as death has claimed many of those who in its early days were among its largest contributors. Among these were Johnson J. Winants, Peter L. Cortelyou, Capt. John Cole, the Rev. Jesse Oakley, Jacob Winant, John V. S. Woglom, Isaac Winant, B. P. Winant, George W. La Forge, Joel B. Ayres, David Morris, John D. Winant and Cornelius J. Winant (moved away). These were all liberal supporters contributing largely of both money and services, and so many deaths have been a severe blow to this little church. But we trust that others will, in time, fill the places thus left vacant, and that St. John's will share in the general prosperity of the Methodist Episcopal churches of Staten Island.

LIST OF PASTORS.

1876-8—Salmon D. Jones, stationed at Stony Point, N. Y.; entered ministry in 1868.

1879-81—George Winsor, died at Milford, Pa., Dec. 28th, 1884, aged 71 years; 45 years in ministry.

1882—W. W. Vanderhoff, stationed at Weehawken, N. J.; entered ministry in 1883.

1883—A. A. Kidder, stationed at Philadelphia; moved from conference.

1884-6—J. A. Kingsbury, supernumerary, residence at Vineland, N. J.; entered ministry in 1868.

1887-8—W. H. McCormick, supernumerary, residence at Dover, N. J.; entered ministry in 1869.

1889-91—Nicholas Vansant, supernumerary, residence at Madison, N. J.; entered ministry in 1842.

1892-4—M. A. Johnston, stationed at Finesville, N. J.; entered ministry in 1893.

1895-6—D. D. Eaton, supernumerary, residence at Binghamton, N. Y.; entered ministry in 1890.

1896-7—A. A. Anderson, entered ministry in 1897.

1898—M. A. Womer, present pastor.

PRESENT OFFICIALS.

TRUSTEES:

H. H. Seguine, president and treasurer; S. W. Benedict, George W. Oakley, J. G. Winant, J. ⸙⸙⸙ nant.

STEWARDS:

H. H. Seguine, recording steward; S. W. Benedict, district steward; George W. Oakley, D. M. Ayres, A. Parsons Turner; stewardesses, Mrs. J. C. Disosway, Miss Mary Cole, Miss Matilda Winant.

PARSONAGE AID SOCIETY:

The parsonage society was organized May 12th, 1890, during the pastorate of the Rev. I. N. Vansant. The work of the society is to collect funds to keep the parsonage in repair and purchase necessary furniture. The first officers were: Mrs. I. N. Vansant, president; Miss Louisa Johnson, vice-president; Miss Magenta Dixon, secretary, and Miss Julia Oakley, treasurer.

The present officers are: Miss Mary Cole, president; Miss Etta Slaight, secretary; Miss Magenta Dixon, treasurer; Miss May Disosway and Miss Matilda Winant, collectors.

SUNDAY-SCHOOL:

The first officers of St. John's Sunday-school were: Capt. John Cole, superintendent and treasurer; Joel Cole, assistant superintendent; John D. Winant, librarian.

The superintendents who have served from its organization are as follows: Capt. John Cole, Jacob Winant, John D. Winant, Joseph C. Winant, Joel B. Ayres, Cornelius J. Winant, James Cortelyou, George W. La Forge, D. M. Ayres.

The present officers are: Winant B. Sharrott, superintendent; Miss Mary Cole, assistant superintendent; Miss Minnie Disosway, secretary; Miss Augusta Ayres, assistant secretary; Mrs. J. C. Disosway, treasurer; Miss Fanny Sharrott, librarian; Miss Magenta Dixon, organist; Miss Augusta Ayres, assistant organist; D. M. Ayres, chorister; Miss Matilda Winant, president and secretary missionary society.

EPWORTH LEAGUE:

The Epworth League was formed in 1893, during the pastorate of the Rev. M. A. Johnston. The first officers were:

Mrs. M. A. Johnston, president; Miss Magenta Dixon, first vice-president; Miss Amelia Dixon, second vice-president; Miss Matilda Johnson, third vice-president; Mrs. Eber Guyon, secretary; Miss Minnie Disosway, treasurer.

The League now has seventy-four members, with the following officers: Rev. M. A. Womer, president; Miss Mary Cole, first vice-president; Miss Matilda Winant, second vice-president; Miss Magenta Dixon, third vice-president; Miss Lorena Bath, secretary; Miss Minnie Disosway, treasurer.

LIST OF PRESENT MEMBERS.

Mr. and Mrs. Samuel W. Benedict.
     "   John S. Burgher.
     "   Louis N. Meyer.
     "   Joseph C. Winant.
     "   H. H. Seguine.
     "   Nathan A. Turner.
     "   Jacob G. Winant.
     "   D. M. Ayres.
Mrs. Sidney N. Post,

S. W. BENEDICT.
Charter Member of St. John's ; Trustee and Steward since
its organization.

Mrs. George Van Schoick.
  " John C. Disosway.
  " William Dixon, Sr.
  " Antonio Thompson.
  " Eva Guyon.
  " Barbara Heldt.
  " Sarah La Forge.
  " Sarah R. Moore.
  " Evelina Ryerson.
  " Caroline Slaight.
Miss Mary Slaight.
  " Emma Slaight.
  " Etta Slaight.
  " Caressa Turner.
  " Maud Van Schoick.
  " Frances M. Winant.
  " Susannah Beyer.
  " Lorena Bath.
  " Mary Cole.
  " Minanetta Disosway.
  " Magenta Dixon.
  " Gabriella La Forge.
Mr. James Mercer.
  " George W. Oakley.
  " Gustavus Rose.
  " Hiram Turner.
  " Parsons Turner.
  " Albert N. Turner.
  " Abram W. Woglom.
  " Everett Vaughan.
  " John Frink.
  " R. W. Dixon, Sr.
  "Thomas P. Hardy.
  " Wesley Kingsland.

A. M. E. ZION CHURCH,

BOGARDUS' CORNERS, NEW YORK.

CHAPTER VIII.

A. M. E. ZION.

BY THE REV. WM. T. BIDDLE.

THE A. M. E. ZION CHURCH was founded in 1850, as a branch of the A. M. E. Zion Church, of New York, the first colored Methodist church in America, which dates back to 1796. The first church was built in 1854, and occupied until the congregation moved to the new church Dec. 19th, 1897, the Sunday before Christmas. The first church was located just off the Bloomingdale road at Bogardus' Corners. It was a plain wooden structure seating about 150 persons. In this old church many interesting meetings have been held, and also many successful revivals.

The organization was formed at a meeting held Dec. 5th, 1850, at the house of William H. Pitts, in Rossville. The first members of the church were Cæsar Jackson, Francis Williams, William Webb, William H. Stevens, John J. Henry, Moses K. Harris, Israel Pitts, Isaac Purnell, Ishmael Robins, Henry Jackson, Elizabeth Titus, Sarah J. Landin, Esther V. S. Purnell, Ann M. Bishop, Grace Williams and Louisa Harris.

The first five named were chosen trustees. The Rev. William H. Pitts was appointed pastor. Meetings were held at the residences of the pastor and of different members of the congregation until the first church edifice was opened in 1854.

The church prospered and grew, and the congregations increased until 1875, when, under the pastorate of the Rev. G. M. Landin, there was a division and a number seceded, forming a new church.

Mr. Landin succeeded the Rev. Louis R. Henry, who died in April 1875, after a successful pastorate of two years. At that time, there was a small society at Port Richmond, and the Rev. John Smith was sent to them as a pastor by the A. M. E. conference.

The congregation refused to receive Mr. Smith, and without waiting for the bishop to act upon the matter, made an arrangement with Mr. Landin, to supply this congregation as well as his own. This, being contrary to the discipline of the church, a charge was presented against Mr. Landin, and Bishop Clinton appointed, as an ecclesiastical court to examine into the case, Elders James Smith, N. R. Turpin, C. Robinson, J. H. White and S. J. Berry.

The trial was held at Port Richmond. Mr. Landin acknowledged that he had made the arrangement charged, but would not admit that he had done wrong nor retract from his position. He was, therefore, expelled from the conference.

Edward Henman, who was then chairman of the board of trustees, was present at the trial and, on his return, made a report to his church upholding Mr. Landin, and representing that he had been expelled unjustly. Many of the congregation sided with Mr. Landin and Mr. Henman. A meeting was

called on July 16th, and, after hearing Mr. Henman's
account of the trial, a resolution was passed that
the church would not receive any other pastor
during the year nor pay any conference claims. A
committee was also sent to Bishop Clinton to protest against the action of the elders in expelling
Mr. Landin. Mr. Henman was made chairman of
the meeting.

On the following Sunday, the committee reported
that Bishop Clinton refused to rescind the action
of the elders and proposed that they secede from
the conference, and when all who wished to sever
their connection were requested to stand, about
two-thirds of the congregation rose.

Deacon Moses K. Harris was then appointed a
delegate to visit the bishop and report the condition
of the church. The bishop sent the Rev. James
Smith, who acted as chairman at the trial of Mr.
Landin, Elder N. R. Turpin, another member of
the trial court, and the secretary, with the minutes,
to explain matters and heal the breach, and explain that Mr. Landin had been guilty in arrang-
ing to supercede the regularly-appointed pastor
of the Port Richmond church, before that pastor
had been relieved or withdrawn by the bishop, and
that he had refused to acknowledge his wrong or
to make any amends for it.

It was impossible, however, to heal the breach,
and fifty-seven of the seventy members went out,
leaving only thirteen with a debt of $477, and the
minister's salary to provide for. These were dark
days for this struggling church. A new board of
trustees was elected from the steadfast members,
August 16th, 1875, consisting of Dawson Landin,

Sr., John Jackson, George Purnell, George W. Bishop and George E. Henman.

In 1890, the trustees purchased from William L. Hinds, one and one-quarter acres on Bloomingdale road, for $650, the site where the new church now stands.

This was during the pastorate of the Rev. E. M. Stanton, and the congregation began at once raising the necessary funds for erecting a new church. The foundation was laid in 1890, during the pastorate of the Rev. F. E. Owens. Mr. Owens remained but one year and was succeeded by the Rev. R. F. Butler. During Mr. Butler's term, it was found that $300 of the money raised for building a new church had disappeared. If the trustees ever found how the loss occurred, or who was responsible for it, it was not made public, or the guilty person punished. This was a severe loss, and for a while the members were completely discouraged. The realization of their hopes for a new place of worship seemed further away than ever, but after a time they decided to renew their efforts and to take such precautions as should prevent any further losses.

The present pastor, the Rev. Wm. T. Biddle, assumed charge of the church in 1894, and infused new life into the little congregation, and by the most strenuous efforts and by help of generous people outside of the church, they succeeded, in 1897, in building the new edifice, and held the first service in it on Dec. 19th. It was largely due to the energy and perseverance of Homer Harris that they were able to erect the new building. The cost of the new church, when it is entirely completed and furnished, will be, including the site, about $5,000.

The old church will still be retained and used for entertainments, festivals, lectures, etc.

The membership of the church is now 48, and there are 88 scholars in the Sunday-school.

LIST OF MINISTERS.

The ministers who have served the church, during the past forty years, are as follows:

William H. Pitts (two terms).

Jeptha Bancroft.

William H. Dumpson (three terms).

Edward Bishop.

Peter Costa.

Isaac Coleman.

William H. Bishop.

John Marshall.

Thomas James.

Lewis R. Henry (two terms).

G. M. Landin.

John Jones (two terms).

G. W. Smith.

Adam Jackson.

Jonah Marshall.

Abraham Anderson (two terms).

E. M. Stanton (four terms).

F. E. Owens (one year).

R. F. Butler (two years).

Wm. T. Biddle (four years).

Among those who have served as class leaders or in the official board, are the following:

Francis Williams, John J. Henry, Charles Bishop, Dawson Landin, Edmund Henman, Ishmael Robins, Eben Bishop, William Purnell, Robert H. Landin,

Sr., Geo. W. Bishop, Robert Landin, Geo. Purnell, Jacob Finny, John Tyler.

The present officers of the church are:

TRUSTEES:

Robert H. Landin, chairman; George W. Bishop, Jr., secretary; Levi Moss, treasurer; Robert Landin, James McCoy, Daniel Green and William Landin.

STEWARDS:

George Purnell, poor steward; John Tyler; board of stewardesses: Mrs. Levi Moss, Mrs. George W. Bishop, Mrs. George E. Henman, Mrs. Samuel Purnell, Mrs. Homer Harris.

EXHORTERS:

Louis Roach and James Decker.

Sunday-school superintendent: James McCoy.

LIST OF MEMBERS.

Mr. and Mrs. Robert H. Landin.
" George W. Bishop.
" Levi Moss.
" Robert Landin.
" James McCoy.
" Wm. D. Landin.
" Daniel Green.
" John Tyler.
" George Purnell.
" Wm. R. Brown.
" Louis Roach.
" Samuel Hammond.
" Benjamin Titus.
" George E. Henman.
" Francis Henny.
" Francis Fish.
" Wm. Pedrom.
" George Henry.

Mr. and Mrs. Homer Harris.
        "   Jacob Finny.
        "   Dawson Landin, Jr.
Mrs. Lucy Cooley.
   " Edith Purnell.
   " Martha Gray.
   " Annie Copeland.
   " Susan Smith.
Miss Emily Tyler.
   " Mamie Bishop.
Mr. Dawson Landin.
  " Charles Moody.
  " Daniel Decker.
  " Benjamin Benedict.
  " John P. Thompson.
  " George Bishop, Jr.
  " John H. Purnell.
  " Alfred Benedict.
  " James Decker.

MT. ZION M. E. CHURCH,

BOGARDUS' CORNERS, NEW YORK.

CHAPTER IX.

MT. ZION.

MT. ZION M. E. CHURCH, on the Bloomingdale road, between Bogardus' Corners and Rossville, was organized in 1875 and was the result of a division in the Mt. Zion A. M. E. Church. It was during the pastorate of the Rev. G. M. Landin. Mr. Landin made arrangements, without first obtaining the consent of the bishop, Bishop Clinton, to supply the Port Richmond charge.

On this account complaint was made to the bishop, who appointed a committee to try the charges. The committee decided against Mr. Landin, and fifty-seven of his parishioners, believing that Mr. Landin had been unjustly dealt with, seceded from the A. M. E. Church and conference and organized the Mt. Zion Church and joined the Newark M. E. conference. Mr. Landin also joined the Newark conference and was made the first pastor of the new congregation. Trustees were elected and a private house was leased for holding services.

Mr. Landin remained two years, and at the end of that period Mt. Zion M. E. Church was attached to the Rossville charge, and for eight years the Rev.

Jesse Oakley, a local preacher living at Rossville, conducted the services.

During the second year of Mr. Oakley's service the trustees purchased of Silas Harris, for $300, the lot, 75x125 feet, where the church and parsonage now stand, and built the present church edifice. The church and lot were all paid for except a debt of $300. In 1885, during the pastorate of the Rev. Ambrose Compton, this debt was paid off through the liberality of the late O. A. Wood, who donated that amount to the church. Mr. Compton served one year and was succeeded by the Rev. William Coombs, who also remained but one year.

In 1887, the church was placed under the charge of the Rev. Wm. H. McCormick, pastor of St. John's M. E. Church, Rossville, who conducted the services until 1889. At the expiration of Mr. McCormick's pastorate at St. John's, Mt. Zion Church was transferred to the Delaware conference, and the Rev. C. J. Hall was sent here. During his pastorate, the present small but comfortable parsonage was built. Mr. Hall remained two years and was succeeded by the Rev. William Brown, who served the church with much acceptability for four years. The Rev. C. J. Gaither was then appointed pastor and remained three years, and until the conference of 1898 appointed the Rev. T. H. White, of Montclair, N. J., to the pastorate.

Among the former trustees, who have served a number of years, are Edward Henman, twenty-one years; Eben Bishop, seventeen years; Charles Bishop, four years; Zedick Pernell, three years; John W. Bishop, three years; John C. Dickerson, three years; William J. Pernell, two years.

The present trustees are: John W. Forsburg, president, who has served seventeen years; Josiah Bishop, treasurer, seventeen years; John Henman, six years; Edward Cole, six years; William J. Bishop, secretary, twenty-three years.

SINKING FUND SOCIETY:

The church has a very efficient sinking fund society whose object is to raise money to defray current expenses and to pay off the small debt on the parsonage.

The present officers are: Rev. John C. Dickerson, president; John Henman, secretary; Mrs. Matilda Roach, treasurer.

SUNDAY-SCHOOL:

The Sunday-school was established immediately on the organization of the church, and has done much good work among the children of the congregation. The superintendents who have had charge of the school from its formation are as follows:

Edward Henman, four years; John W. Forsburg, two years; Vincent Lindsey, two years; John C. Dickerson, one year; John Henman, the present superintendent, fourteen years.

PRESENT MEMBERSHIP.

The present membership of this church includes:
Mr. and Mrs. Vincent Lindsey.
"   John C. Dickerson.
"   Edward Henman.
"   Edward Cole.
"   John W. Bishop.
"   David Morse.
"   John W. Forsburg.
"   Daniel Bland.
"   Thomas Williams.

Mrs. Samuel Fish.
    "   Joseph Bishop.
    "   John Mangin.
    "   Vincent Pervis.
    "   Nellie Decker.
    "   Mary J. Bishop.
    "   Ellen Conover.
    "   Matilda Roach.
    "   Louisa Dumpson.
    "   Hannah Pernell.
    "   Elizabeth Gregory.
    "   Susan Bell.
Miss Mamie Bland.
    "   Jane Bishop.
    "   Lulu Bland.
    "   Florence Bishop.
    "   Susan J. Bishop.
Mr. Littleton Johnson.
    "   Josiah Bishop.
    "   William H. Bishop.
    "   John H. Henman.
    "   John E. Bishop.
    "   William A. Bishop.

ASBURY M. E. CHURCH,

NEW SPRINGVILLE, NEW YORK.

ASBURY M. E. CHURCH.
New Springville.

CHAPTER X.

THE first entry in the church records of the Asbury Methodist Episcopal Church is as follows:

" The Methodist Episcopal Church, in the township of Northfield and county of Richmond and state of New York, was built in the year of our Lord 1802."

Then follows the certificate of the first election of trustees: "This is to certify, that on the 30th day of January, 1803, there was an election held at the house of Nicholas Crocheron, Esq., for the purpose of choosing trustees. After choosing Nicholas Crocheron, Esq., and Richard Merrell, to preside at said election, they proceeded to choose James Wood, John Decker, Nicholas Crocheron, Richard Merrell and the Rev. Elias Price (a local preacher), trustees. They were elected by a plurality of votes to take charge of all the temporalities belonging to the Methodist Episcopal Church, in the township of Northfield, county of Richmond, and state of New York, and the name and style by which they are known and distinguished is ' The trustees of the Methodist Episcopal Church in the township of Northfield, county of Richmond, and state of New York.'

"Given under our hands and seals the day and year above mentioned.

JAMES C. WOOD, JOHN DECKER,	} First class.
NICHOLAS CROCHERON, RICHARD MERRELL,	} Second class.
ELIAS PRICE,	} Third class."

The history of the church of course antedates this record, but the only means of ascertaining the efforts prior to this record is through the information handed down to the present generation by their ancestors.

The oldest of these, and the one who has been most intimately identified with the Asbury Church for the past seventy-five years, is the Rev. John B. Hillyer, whose father often entertained the itinerant ministers of the Methodist church on their journey through the Island from the old Blazing Star ferry (in Rossville) to Mersereau's ferry (Port Richmond). Many of the facts which we here give of the history of the beginning of the old Neck Church (now Asbury) we glean from Mr. Hillyer, who well remembers the families of Messrs. Hillyer, Price, Morgan, Crocheron, Simonson, Decker and other members of that little society which formed the nucleus of the first Methodist Episcopal church in Northfield.

We are unable to learn just where and by whom the first Methodist services were held in the district which later comprised the Long Neck charge, but it is probable that some services were held at private houses very shortly after Francis Asbury made his first visit to Staten Island. The pastors appointed to New Jersey were accustomed to make occasional visits to Staten Island and, during their absence, meetings were held by the local preachers. Among the first of these were William Cole, Joseph Totten and Elias Price. These services were held sometimes in private houses and sometimes in the school-houses, and the farmers used to take their large wagons with their horses or oxen, gather up a load of their less fortunate neighbors, and drive for miles over the rough country roads, and many would walk from Mariners' Harbor and Port Richmond, morning and evening, and neither storm nor mud kept them from the service.

Notwithstanding all these discouragements and difficulties, or perhaps on account of them, the society continued to grow and flourish and, in 1802, when the church was built, the society numbered 64 members. This was the second Methodist Episcopal church on Staten Island, and was located near the site of the present Asbury M. E. Church.

At this time the church was under the pastorate of the Rev. Caleb B. Pedicord and the Rev. Joseph Cromwell, of the East Jersey district. Mr. John Hillyer was the first secretary of the board of trustees.

The second entry in the record gives the names of the members belonging to the Methodist Episcopal Church at the time the church was built in 1802-3. They are as follows:

Elias Price, class leader. Jane Decker.
John Morgan. Lydia Decker.
Nicholas Crocheron, Jr. Tabitha Blake.
James Decker. Esther Houghwout.
Moses Decker. Gettie Simonson.
Matthias Decker. Mary Decker.
John Simonson. Nancy Cannon.
Silas Reynolds. Elizabeth Price.

Richard Decker.
Matthias Decker, Sr.
John Cannon.
Benjamin Price.
Abraham Decker.
Thomas Decker.
Isaac Decker.
James Wood.
David Decker.
Sylvanus Decker.
John Decker.
Richard Decker.
Richard Merrell, Jr.
David Price.
Aaron Decker.
Daniel Price.
Richard Merrell, Sr.
Robert Simonson.
Thomas Decker.
Abraham Simonson.
Jacob Van Pelt.
John Wood.
Susannah Morgan.
Anna Crocheron.
Jemima Decker.

Catharine Decker.
Mary Decker.
Sarah Decker.
Mary Ann Decker.
Ann Crocheron.
Martha Merrell.
Suzanna Wood.
Elsie Hillyer.
Margaret Merrell.
Rebekah Reynolds.
Hannah Bowman.
Maryan Decker.
Maysy Wood.
Anna Simonson.
Polly Laroza.
Abigail Laroza.
Mary Curron.
Mary Van Pelt.
Anne Decker.
Mary Bowman.

COLORED.

Men.

Pompey.
Jack.

Women.

Rose.
Margaret.
Grace.

From the opening of the church in 1803, until 1810, this church, as well as all the Methodist services held on the Island, was under the pastorates of the Elizabethtown and Staten Island ministers. In 1810, Thomas Drummond was sent to Staten Island, and had charge of Woodrow and Asbury, the only two Methodist Episcopal churches on Staten Island. He was followed by Jacob Hevener, Sylvester Hill, John Robertson and James Polhemus,

MRS. CATHERINE DECKER.
The oldest Methodist on Staten Island; aged 91.

each of whom remained one year. During this time, the Staten Island churches were not prosperous, and it seemed best to rely largely upon local preachers. Therefore, in 1815, the Island was made a part of the Essex, N. J., charge, and remained so for eleven years. The old Tabernacle, now Bethel Church, had been built in 1822, and, in 1826, the conference decided to make Staten Island a separate charge, and appointed Bartholomew Weed pastor over the three churches—Woodrow, Asbury and Bethel.

In 1840, three new churches having been built within the previous year, or two, the Island was divided into two parishes, the Rev. Isaac Cross being sent to the Northfield circuit, including Asbury, Port Richmond, Mariners' Harbor and Quarantine, and the Rev. Daniel Parish to Westfield (Woodrow and Bethel). Mr. Cross, having four churches under his charge, was assisted by the Rev. Elias Price and the Rev. Inman Hall, local preachers, and occasional visits from clergymen from New York and vicinity.

From the year 1815, Asbury Church seems to have been in a more prosperous financial condition. In that year, it paid all its debts and had a considerable balance in the treasury, and from that time on, we find in the statement frequently recurring in the reports of the treasurer, that all bills had been paid, with a few pounds (sterling) remaining in the treasury.

The period from 1835 to 1842 seems to have been a church-building period among the Methodists of Staten Island. In 1838, the first Kingsley Church was built; in 1839, the Summerfield and Trinity; in

1841, the Tabernacle people built a new church (the old Bethel which was burned in 1886), and the same year the old Woodrow Church was torn down and the present edifice erected. These new churches, two in Westfield, two in Northfield and one at Stapleton, stirred up the spirit of improvement in old Asbury, and, in 1849, during the pastorate of the Rev. L. R. Dunn, the trustees purchased from Daniel G. Crocheron, for $500, one and one-fourth acres adjoining the old church, and erected the first brick church on Staten Island, about 200 feet north of the site of the old church.

The old church was built by the late John B. Hillyer. It was about 32x38 feet and stood with the side to the road and the front door facing the south. When arrangements were made to build a new church, the old building was sold, for $200, to the late Enos Van Pelt, by whom it was moved to Butcherville, and remodeled into a dwelling. The last service held in the old church was the funeral of the late John Depuy, Nov. 22nd, 1849.

For the following description of the old church we are indebted to the pen of I. J. Simonson, one of the prominent members of both the old and the new churches:

"The church was quaint in appearance, being almost square. The outside of the church was covered with shingles, which, after many years of exposure, had changed their color. The interior of the church was in keeping with the exterior. The seats were made after the pattern of a large shoe box, with the cover off and one side knocked out. They were formerly painted white, but had changed with age to a darker color. Here and there a red-

breasted knot would be looking at one as he vainly
tried to shut out all objects from his devotion.
Along the top edge of the seats was painted a fine
red line, to break the monotony of the shoe-box
architecture. One soon lost sight of the seats as
he gazed at the chancel-rail that surrounded the
altar. The rail was three inches square, and the
edges were beveled. The uprights were fully four
feet high, square and straight, as if to remind those
who approached them of the square rule of life and
the upright character of the people.

"The pulpit was—Who can describe it? Supported by four columns, leaving ample room for the
devout women who wished to attend the service,
but who had no one to care for the babies. But
here was a place where the babies were safe and
free from all harm. After ascending some ten or
twelve steps one was on a level with the speaker's
stand. Here enclosed on every side by a high
breastwork stood the minister, fearless and bold,
because no one could go near him unless the pulpit
was carried by storm. Overhead was a large sound-
ing-board, so that the voice of the preacher could
be heard in the rear of the church, which was 36
feet long.

"The trustees, thinking at the time when the
church was built, that there might come a time
when more room would be needed, had a gallery
run on three sides, which, with the sounding-
board on the other end, left just room for those in
the gallery to look below. Here the choir was
placed—that is, when there was one, which, like the
chills and fever, came periodically. When there
was no choir to lead the singing, it was amusing to

see the different leaders of music put forth their best efforts and make even the old boards of the seats whiz with the harmony. Sometimes all the leaders would try, one after another, to get the tune well adjusted to harmony, but would most of the time fail; and the minister would help out the service with a lengthy prayer.

"The right side of the church was reserved for women and the left side for men. A dog could go on the right side if he did not bark, but a male member of the congregation could not, unless he had the contribution plate in his hand, and then with a weird face and measured step he took the 'cents of the meeting.' The women wore straw bonnets, projecting well over the face, tied with ribbons which cost a penny a yard, and that was all the ornament worn of any sort. Shy glances at times would quiver like a ray of sunshine for a moment and then retreat, and happy was the young fellow that had been on the watch for this flickering comfort.

"Sunday was a gala day (or evening) of the week. When church service was ended every man that had an overcoat was sure to have his fists stuck in the sleeves and extended in a direction to meet the head of his neighbor, and by the time the 'Old Hundred' was over each man and coat had become reconciled to each other's company.

"Outside the church were the lads arranged in order, according to the intensity of their affections. The old lover came first, and so down to the timid, bashful lad who had not courage to ask his girl's permission to see her safely home, but waited in the dark to cover up his want of valor. Sometimes he got the slip, for a more fortunate fellow was ahead of him. The older people left the church more slowly, for it was necessary to cool off after the exertion of the evening, and to keep themselves from taking cold, that they might be in 'good voice' for the next evening. Those who had little children with them would awaken them from their sleep and kiss the little darlings for keeping so quiet and allowing their parents to do all the shouting.

"But with all their eccentricities these people paid dollar for dollar. They helped the poor in their afflictions, took good care of their pastor, and when many of these actors were laid away, when the light of this life went out, when their journey was done, when their earthly meetings were over, they went to their reward where worth of character is fully appreciated."

Unfortunately, all the records containing the accounts of the rebuilding of the church in 1849, have been lost or destroyed, and we are only able to give such facts as we can glean from memoranda in the possession of John B. Hillyer, and from the recollection of the old members of the church, who can give the principal facts, but, of course, not exact dates and figures.

The new church was built in 1849, during the pastorate of the Rev. L. R. Dunn, by a mason named Riker, of Newark, N. J., and J. L. Richards, carpenter. The new church was 45x60 feet, with a broad gallery running across the front, and furnished seating accommodations for about 400.

In 1845, during the pastorate of the Rev. W. A. Wilmer, the trustees purchased from John Q. Simonson, for $400, the present parsonage lot and the small house that was then standing upon it. In 1858, a part of the house was torn down, and the present parsonage built, at a cost of about $1,500, $1,000 of which was raised at the time, by subscriptions. The same year the church was papered and the wood-work grained, at a considerable cost.

The congregation had been greatly weakened by the building of the Mariners' Harbor and Trinity churches in 1839, and having spent a large amount of money in building the new church and parsonage, had been for a long time in debt, but they determined, in 1866, to make a strong effort to free the church from the debt on which they had been paying interest for nearly twenty years. In this, they were successful, and in one year were able to take up all outstanding obligations.

The following year, during the pastorate of the Rev. A. H. Belles, $150 was spent in repainting and repairing the parsonage, and, in 1871, $300 was expended for new carpets, mattings, stoves, pulpit trimmings and other improvements to the church.

The first official action taken in the matter of the remodeling of the church, was a resolution passed by the board of trustees, June 23rd, 1873, appointing Isaac Winant and O. J. Prall a committee to solicit subscriptions, work to be begun when $2,500 had been subscribed. The estimated cost of the improvements then under consideration was about $6,000. Collectors were appointed, the charge was divided into districts, and a thorough canvass was made. When the committee made their report two months later, they had been able to raise little more than half of the proposed $2,500, and the work was postponed until the following year.

The next year new plans were drawn, reducing the cost to $4,800, but it was found impossible, this being the year of the panic and the hard times that followed the financial crisis of 1873, to raise the money. The work was still further postponed and nothing was accomplished until 1878.

In 1877, that portion of the front wall above the columns at the entrance, and which was built of pressed brick, unburned, fell out, breaking the flagging of the front walk, and blocked the entrance to the church. This was a condition of affairs which could not long be borne by a congregation which took as much pride in its house of worship as the members of old Asbury have always taken, and as times had somewhat improved, it was determined, in spite of all obstacles, not only to repair the front, but to make other improvements which had been in contemplation.

With this determination in view, at a meeting of the board held Sept. 5th, 1878, I. J. Simonson, Abraham Crocheron and Isaac Winant, were appointed a committee to procure definite plans and specifications and submit the same to the board. At the next meeting, held Sept. 9th, 1878, the plans were approved, and the committee instructed to proceed with the work. Mr. Simonson found a builder who offered to put in a new front for $1,250. This offer was accepted without hesitation. This $1,250 could only provide for the work that was actually necessary, with the cheapest materials, but the trustees felt confident that if the improvements were once begun, public interest would be aroused and the friends and members of the church would furnish the means to beautify, as well as to protect, the building. In this, they were not mistaken. As soon as the church people saw that the building was to be disfigured with a front of common brick, they demanded that sufficient be added to provide Philadelphia front brick. The plans were also changed to build a bell tower over the front entrance and insert front windows of figured glass. The gallery was taken out, a recess built in the rear for the choir, the walls were kalsomined and the wood-work repainted and many minor improvements were made, so that when the work was finished, it was found that $3,200 had been expended instead of $1,250, as first proposed. This had nearly all been raised on subscription, and the deficiency was raised by the trustees on two notes of $400 each, which were paid shortly afterward.

All that the congregation now lacked was a bell They had a tower, but no bell to call the worshipers together, and the congregation that had bravely borne all the past expenses felt that they would have to postpone the purchase of this much-needed article.

At this juncture, two friends, Olin M. Barber and John W. Collins, took the matter in hand and, outside of the congregation, raised $450 and presented the church with the 1400-pound bell which now hangs in the tower.

This large expenditure had put the church property in excellent condition, but placed the trustees in debt to the amount of $800. Little of historical interest occurred from that time until 1897, with the exception of an expenditure of $350 for improvements, stoves, etc., in 1884, and such events as appear under their appropriate heads.

In 1897, during the first year of the pastorate of the Rev. John McMurray, $1,050 was spent in improvements. The walls and ceiling were decorated, new carpets laid, the church was furnished throughout with handsome new·oak pews, and lighted by electricity. On October 10th, the church was rededicated. Three services were held, the pastor preaching at he morning service, the Rev. W. H. McCormick in the afternoon, and Presiding Elder George W. Smith in the evening.

The Ladies' Aid Society provided the money to purchase the carpet ($178), the sum of $372 was collected on subscriptions and $415 was pledged at the three services.

The officials, members and friends of old Asbury are now looking forward to the celebration of its one-hundredth anniversary, which will probably be the next important event in its history.

REMINISCENCES OF OLD ASBURY BY THE OLDEST METHODIST ON STATEN ISLAND.

Mrs. Catherine Decker is one of the most remarkable old ladies on Staten Island. She was born near Mariners' Harbor in 1806, and though ninety-two years of age is able to quote whole chapters from the Bible and repeat hymns she heard sung at the prayer-meetings over sixty years ago.

She distinctly remembers going to the little frame school-house near her home eighty-eight years ago. We can well believe that her teachers were not graduates of the Normal schools.

Eighty years ago she used to go with her mother to the old Neck (now Asbury) Church, walking three miles through the woods and back, often at night.

She says that her mother and other women of the neighborhood would, after a hard day's labor, doing all the work for a family of six or eight children, and without a sewing-machine either, sit down in the afternoon to their sewing and begin discussing neighborhood affairs, principally the meetings which were the chief source of interest in that quiet locality. Finally, one would announce that she "would like to go to the meeting to-night to hear the minister from New Jersey." The others would express the same wish and the final conclusion would be that they would have an early supper and then all start out with their husbands for a three-mile walk through the woods to the meeting.

Mrs. Decker recollects many interesting and amusing incidents of the early days of emotional Methodism. One old lady, a Mrs. Katherine Decker, wife of David Decker, would rise, during the sermon, and clap her hands and shout, so that the good dominie was often obliged to stop his discourse. Sometimes he would sit down and wait until she had finished, and would then resume the thread of his sermon.

Among the prominent Methodists of those old days whom Mrs. Decker well remembers were the local preachers, Elias Price, James C. Wood and William Cole; John Braisted, the class leader, who used to sing with great unction:

> "O how good it is to be blessed,
>   And dwell where Jesus is
> Jesus now is passing by,
>   Calls the mourners to him.
> He has died for you and I:
>   Only look and follow him.
> Streaming mercy how it flows,
>   For I know and feel it.
> Half has never yet been told,
>   Still I want to tell it;"

and Jacob Braisted, a local preacher, who used to go
to the church through the severest storms, and if
the building were not opened he would stand on the
sheltered side during the regular hour for service
and would say that he was as greatly blessed as if
he had heard a sermon.

The camp-meetings of this period, Mrs. Decker
says, brought many converts to Methodism. These
were often held in the woods near Watchoaks
(Bloomfield). The people used to come from all
parts of the Island and from New Jersey. Those
who lived too far away to return home at night
would bring tents and many of them would stay,
with their families, the entire week of the meeting.

Mrs. Decker attended the Asbury Church until
the Mariners' Harbor Church (now Summerfield)
was built. Her mother gave the first five dollars
toward the erection of this church, and after it
was finished Mrs. Decker joined it, as it was nearer
her home than the Asbury. She has been a member of this church over sixty years.

Mrs. Decker has heard many of the famous early
apostles of Methodism in America, but the occasion
which she most cherishes in her memory is the
last sermon preached by the Rev. "Father" Boehm.
It was at the conference of 1875, shortly before his
death, and she remembers the text: "The Lord is
Merciful."

As an instance of Mrs. Decker's wonderful
memory, she is able to give the text, chapter and
verse of a sermon preached by the Rev. Mr. Farth-
ing in 1826: Deut. xxiii, 24.

Mrs. Decker was deeply attached to her mother
and often remarks on the similarity of their lives,

Both were married at the age of seventeen and to husbands seven years older than themselves; both were left widows at thirty-eight, with seven children, the youngest in each case being only two years of age. Mrs. Decker's mother lived to the age of ninety-three and Mrs. Decker is convinced that she will live to the same age.

She still lives, and always has, in the house built for his bride by her husband seventy-four years ago. She lives all alone, does her own work, and is as cheerful and happy as when a young girl under her father's roof.

DICKINSON CHAPEL.

THE first Methodist Episcopal chapel at Travis-ville was built in 1842, on a site donated by the late Abraham Decker. The place was called Long Neck, and this was known as the Long Neck Church.

Previous to that time services were held at the houses of different members, usually at that of John Wood, who was a class leader and exhorter. This house, the cradle of Methodism in Travisville, was on the site now occupied by the residence of Cornelius Leonard.

The chapel was occupied as a place of worship until about the year 1868, when it was sold to school district No. 3, of Northfield, for a school-house. Services were still held in the school-house for some time after it had been sold, as there was considerable delay in building the new chapel.

The records of this first chapel seem to have been lost, for the first record we can find of the official board was of a meeting held in the school-house, the Rev. George F. Dickinson, pastor of the Asbury charge, presiding. Daniel T. Depuy was chosen secretary.

This meeting was called to take some action in regard to building a new church or chapel, and the following were elected trustees of the proposed new church: Silas R. Decker, William P. Decker, Raymond Decker, David R. Decker and Daniel T. Depuy. A resolution was also passed that the new church should be named the Dickinson Methodist Episcopal Church, of Long Neck, in honor of the pastor.

At the organization of the board of trustees, William P. Decker was elected president, Daniel T. Depuy, secretary, and Silas R. Decker, treasurer.

The site for the new church was purchased January 4th, 1866, of Silas R. Decker, for $400, but as Mr. Decker donated $100 of the purchase price the net cost was only $300.

At a meeting of the trustees held at the house of David R. Decker, May 28th, 1866, the trustees adopted the plans for a chapel 29x42 feet, enclosed in perpendicular Gothic style. No further steps were taken until April 24th, 1867, when David R. Decker and Daniel T. Depuy were appointed a committee to secure estimates for building the church, under the plans previously adopted. Nicholas Decker and Stephen Crocheron, being the lowest bidders, were awarded the contract.

Much delay was occasioned in raising the necessary funds and the corner-stone was not laid until 1871. The building committee consisted of David R. Decker, William P. Decker, Henry C. Morgan, Charles C. Decker and Nicholas Decker.

The church was finished in the fall of 1871 and

cost about $3,000. The church has always been a chapel under the charge of the pastors of Asbury M. E. Church, of New Springville. The members and congregation, who have always c ontributed liberally to the expenses of the mother church, have kept their chapel in good repair and made frequent improvements, the latter of which was the lighting by electricity.

The first chapel, after the new school-house was built, was sold to the Lutherans and is still used as a place of worship.

Of the original board of trustees, elected in 1865 to build and have charge of the new church, only Raymond Decker is living, and he has served continuously from that time, a period of thirty-three years.

PRESENT OFFICIALS.

TRUSTEES:

John R. Minto, president; David D. Decker, secretary; Louis W. Lowe, treasurer; Raymond Decker, Oscar L. Decker, J. Howard Decker, G. B. Fancher, Isaac J. Reed, Elias P. Decker.

LADIES' AID SOCIETY:

This society was organized on the 2nd of September, 1875, and the following were the first officers:

Mrs. C. D. Price, president; Mrs. E. Decker, vice-president; Miss Fanny M. Decker, secretary; Mrs. Almer Decker, treasurer. The present officers are:

Mrs. C. D. Price, president; Mrs. William Simmonds, vice-president; Mrs. E. A. Decker, secretary; Mrs. Mary A. Decker, treasurer.

SUNDAY-SCHOOL:

The Sunday-school of Dickinson Church was organized in 1858, and has a membership of 156. The officers are:

Louis W. Lowe, superintendent; Mrs. William Simmonds and J. Howard Decker, assistant superintendents; Irving Reed, secretary; John Moffatt, assistant secretary; John Minto, treasurer; William Minto, librarian; Thomas Larson, assistant librarian; Mrs. Edward Demarest, organist; Miss May Minto, chorister.

EPWORTH LEAGUE:

This chapter was formed March 3rd, 1890, and has a membership of 42. The first officers were:

Rev. A. M. Harris, president; D. D. Decker, first vice-president; James Grant, second vice-president; Mrs. S. B. Price, third vice-president; Miss Sadie Decker, fourth vice-president; J. R. Minto, secretary; Mrs. William Simmonds, treasurer.

The present officials are:

J. R. Minto, president; George F. De Vol, first vice-president; Miss Hobie Cannon, second vice-president; Miss Bella Minto, third vice-president; Mrs. William Simmonds, fourth vice-president; Miss May Minto, secretary; Miss Minnie Ferguson, treasurer.

JUNIOR EPWORTH LEAGUE:

The Junior Epworth League was formed in 1890, October 9th, and the first officers were as follows:

Mrs. William Simmonds, president; Mrs. Leonard, vice-president; Fred. Cottier, secretary; John Minto, treasurer.

The present officers:

Mrs. William Simmonds, president; Rev. John McMurray, pastor; Miss May Pettit, secretary; Miss Margaret Schmand, treasurer.

BLOOMFIELD CHAPEL.

BLOOMFIELD CHAPEL is the youngest daughter of Methodism on Staten Island. The first step toward building this chapel was taken at a meeting held July 5th, 1884, at the residence of Cornelius C. Merrell

At this meeting, the following board of trustees was elected: John M. Hughes, Charles D. Merrell, Isaac M. Merrell, Cornelius C. Merrell and Solomon S. Braisted. Mr. Hughes was chosen president, Charles D. Merrell, treasurer, and Isaac M. Merrell, secretary.

The contract for building the new church was awarded to B. Breitung, of Travisville. The site was a free gift from Joseph Ball. The corner-stone of the church was laid in July 1885, and the church was dedicated October 25th, 1885, Bishop Harris officiating at both services.

The church cost about $1,200, all of which has been paid.

Like Dickinson Church, the Bloomfield Church, although it has a separate board of trustees, is conducted as a chapel to Asbury Church. It has a fine Sunday-school of about forty scholars.

TRUSTEES:

John M. Hughes, president; Isaiah Merrell, secretary; S. S. Braisted, treasurer; Calvin E. Bush, Selleck Decker.

LIST OF PASTORS.

For the names of pastors before the Island was divided into separate charges, see Woodrow.

1842—Isaac N. Felch, died at Hackettstown, N. J., March 24th, 1876, aged 69 years; 45 years in ministry.

1843-4—George Hitchens, died Aug. 27th, 1895, aged 80 years; 51 years in ministry.

1845-6—William A. Wilmer, died March 10th, 1878, aged 73 years; 31 years in ministry.

1847-8—Abraham Owen, died Aug. 1st, 1875, aged 75 years; 31 years in ministry.

1849—Lewis R. Dunn, superannuate, residence at East Orange, N. J.; entered ministry in 1841.

1850-1—John N. Crane, died in Newark, N. J., July 9th, 1892, aged 81 years; 59 years in the ministry.

1852-3—Thomas W. Pearson, died at New Providence, N. J., May 28th, 1860, aged 56 years; 35 years in ministry.

1854—Henry Boehm, died at Woodrow, N. Y., Dec. 28th, 1875, aged 100 years; 74 years in ministry.

1855—Henry B. Beegle, died at Ocean Grove, N. J.; March 20th, 1882, aged 71 years; 34 years in ministry.

1856-7—Bartholomew Weed, died in Newark, N. J., Jan. 5th, 1879, aged 86 years: 62 years in ministry.

1858-9—Thomas W. Pearson. (See above).

1860-1—David Walters, superannuate, residence at Lebanon, N. J.; entered ministry in 1852.

1862—J. E. Switzer.

1863-5—George F. Dickinson, stationed in Newark, N. J.; entered ministry in 1854.

1866-8—Amos H. Belles, died in Newark, N. J., April 22nd, 1891, aged 75 years; 42 years in ministry.

1869-70—Peter D. Day, died at New Providence, N. J., Oct. 10th, 1888, aged 77 years; 56 years in ministry.

1871—James M. Tuttle, died at Spring Lake, N. J.,

Nov. 22nd, 1887, aged 78 years; 51 years in ministry.

1872-4—Henry J. Hayter, supernumerary, residence at Bradley Beach, N. J.; entered ministry in 1856.

1875-8—William H. McCormick, supernumerary, residence at Dover, N. J.; entered ministry in 1869.

1878-80—John Faull, died at Sergeantsville, N. J., Feb. 4th, 1887, aged 66 years; 37 years in ministry.

1881—Albert Van Deusen, stationed at Clinton, N. J.; entered ministry in 1866.

1882—Jacob P. Dailey, died at Bethlehem, Pa., April 10th, 1883, aged 63 years; 38 years in ministry.

1883-5—Charles E. Walton, stationed at Flanders, N. J.; entered ministry in 1859.

1886-8—John F. Dodd, secretary of Newark conference, 150 Fifth avenue, New York; entered ministry in 1858.

1889-93—A. M. Harris, stationed at New Providence, N. J.; entered ministry in 1866.

1894-6—W. W. Vanderhoff, stationed at Union Place, N. J.; entered ministry in 1883.

1897—John McMurray, present pastor; entered ministry in 1892.

PRESENT OFFICIALS.

TRUSTEES:

Isaac Winant, president; George M. Christopher, secretary; Minard W. Depuy, treasurer; William Van Pelt, Frank Van Pelt, Crowell Depuy, John D. Blake.

STEWARDS:

Enos F. Depuy, recording steward; Raymond

Decker, district steward; Isaac Winant, George M. Christopher, M. W. Depuy, Crowell Depuy, David D. Decker, John R. Minto, W. P. Hughes, John K. Bush, W. Irving Morgan, J. B. Hillyer, Oscar L. Decker.

LOCAL PREACHERS:

Rev. John E. Hillyer, Rev. Chas. Hunt, Rev. Enos F. Depuy, Rev. James Howard Decker, Rev. James Grant.

LADIES' AID SOCIETY:

The Asbury Ladies' Aid Society was organized Aug. 17th, 1897, with 23 members. This number has rapidly increased, and 55 names now appear on the roll. The society has four departments, with the vice-presidents as chairmen, as follows: First, Pastor's aid; second, Church and Parsonage aid; third, Temperance and Humane work; fourth, Social work.

The officers are:

Mrs. Howard N. Winant, president; Miss Carrie Van Pelt, first vice-president; Mrs. Isaac Winant, second vice-president; Mrs. Henry F. Decker, third vice-president; Mrs. Robert J. Halliday, fourth vice-president; Miss Minnie Martin, secretary; Mrs. George M. Christopher, treasurer.

SUNDAY-SCHOOL:

The Sunday-school was organized in 1823, by the late Reuben Simonson, and his son-in-law, William Ross. The records, with the exception of those from 1860 to 1876, can not be found, and, therefore, we are unable to give a complete list of the superintendents.

The present officers are:

George M. Christopher, superintendent; Willard D. Decker, assistant superintendent; Frank Van-

Pelt, secretary; Isaac Winant, treasurer; George Shotwell, librarian; Isaac Winant, Jr., assistant librarian; Mrs. Charles W. Mesier, organist.

EPWORTH LEAGUE:

Asbury Epworth League, Chapter 850, was organized during the pastorate of the Rev. A. M. Harris, in 1889, and has 40 members. The first officers were: Rev. A. M. Harris, president; Charles Hunt, first vice-president; Miss Jennie Christopher, second vice-president; Mrs. Louisa Zeluff, third vice-president; Miss Ida Simonson, fourth vice-president; Miss Carrie Van Pelt, secretary; Enos Depuy, treasurer.

The present officers consist of the following: Enos F. Depuy, president; George M. Christopher, first vice-president; Mrs. Isaac H. Winant, second vice-president; Mrs. Charles W. Mesier, third vice-president; Miss Minnie Martin, fourth vice-president; Miss Carrie Van Pelt, secretary; Willard D. Decker, treasurer.

JUNIOR EPWORTH LEAGUE:

The Junior Epworth League was organized in 1898 and has 31 members.

Officers: Miss Carrie VanPelt, superintendent; Miss Mamie Prall, president; Miss Shirley Depuy, first vice-president; Miss Lizzie Decker, second vicepresident; Miss Stella Beasley, third vice-president; Miss Lottie Decker, fourth vice-president; Miss Clara Martling, secretary; Fred. Beasley, treasurer.

PRESENT MEMBERSHIP.

The following is the present membership of Asbury Church and Dickinson and Bloomfield chapels:

Mr. and Mrs. John D. Blake.
       "   William R. Blake.
       "   Simpson S. Braisted.
       "   John K. Bush.
       "   Peter S. Cannon.
       "   George M. Christopher.
       "   Raymond Decker.
       "   Willard D. Decker.
       "   David D. Decker.
       "   Nicholas Decker.
       "   Courtland A. Decker.
       "   Sylvanus S. Decker.
       "   Elias P. Decker.
       "   Minard W. Depuy.
       "   Crowell Depuy.
       "   Isaac Houghwout.
       "   John M. Hughes.
       "   Charles Hunt.
       "   Henry Landman.
       "   Oscar L. Decker.
       "   J. Howard Decker.
       "   John William Decker.
       "   Fred. M. Depuy.
       "   Isaiah Merrell.
       "   Leonard A. Merrell.
       "   John R. Minto.
       "   James A. Morgan.
       "   Oscar J. Prall.
       "   Isaac J. Reed.
       "   Irving R. Reed.
       "   Isaac J. Simonson.
       "   John Turnpenny.
       "   William Van Pelt.
       "   William B. Vreeland.

Mr. and Mrs. Isaac Winant.
    "   Howard N. Winant.
    "   Isaac H. Winant.
    "   William Milton Zeluff.
Mrs. Otto A. E. Woehrle.
  " Conrad Zeucher.
  " Robert J. Halliday.
  " Henry Purdy.
  " Rodney Taylor.
  " John E. Abrahams.
  " Richard D. Beasley.
  " Claude Van Pelt.
  " Emiel Bowers.
  " John W. Decker, Sr.
  " John W. Lisk.
  " John McMurray.
  " John W. Decker, Jr.
  " Elsworth Decker.
  " Gilbert A. Depuy.
  " Monteith Eadie.
  " Henry F. Decker.
  " William Edkins.
  " Caleb V. N. Decker.
  " Vanderbilt Decker.
  " Sylvanus S. Decker.
  " Robert Ferguson.
  " William Hunt.
  " James Harrington.
  " James K. Latcheum.
  " William E. Decker.
  " Freeman Blake.
  " Ephraim Decker.
  " George B. Decker.
  " Charles Stevens.

Mrs. Christopher C. Decker.
" Henry E. Pelcher.
" Cornelius Scholes.
" William Simmonds.
" James B. Miller.
" Archie Minto.
" Charles W. Mesier.
" James Moffatt.
" Alfred G. Pearce.
" Charles Simonson.
" Mary M. Pettit.
" Catherine Paull.
" Catharine Price.
" Christiana Simpson.
" Eathilyn A. Merrell.
" Sarah J. Merrell.
" Sarah E. Miller.
" Anna Simonson.
" Josephine Sofield.
" Asenath Bedell.
" Lillie A. Jones.
" Sophronia Decker.
" Louisa Decker.
" Lucy Ann Decker.
" Elizabeth S. Johnson
" Elsie M. Van Pelt.
" Eliza Ann Decker.
" Sarah Shotwell.
" Catharine A. Decker.
" Mary E. Merrell.
" Emma Jane Beasley.
" Sarah Jane Braisted.
" Parmelia A. Cannon.
" Rachel M. Cannon.

Mrs. Catharine J. Christopher.
  " Sarah E. Conley.
  " Mary Ann Crawford.
  " Catherine Crocheron.
  " Alice O. Debow.
  " Elsie Decker.
  " Catherine E. Decker.
  " Harriet Lowe.
  " Mary Frances Decker.
  " Catherine Ann Decker.
  " Mahala Ann Decker.
Miss Lorena Braisted.
  " Mary R. Cannon.
  " Margaret S. Cannon.
  " Alice Christopher.
  " Luella Christopher.
  " Maud M. Chambers.
  " Florence E. Decker.
  " Pauline E. Decker.
  " Geraldine C. Depuy.
  " Christella E. McMurray.
  " Anna McLarty.
  " Mary A. Ferguson.
  " Mary Fisher.
  " Maud M. Houghwout.
  " Mary C. Hughes.
  " Lizzie Hunt.
  " Grace T. Loblein.
  " Maggie Merrell.
  " Juliette A. Merrell.
  " Jennie Mersereau.
  " Bella T. Minto.
  " Nellie Minto.
  " Marjory W. Minto.

Miss Rebecca McFarland.
   " Clara Peterson.
   " Sarah C. Prall.
   " Josephine Price.
   " Sadie M. Reed.
   " Caroline Van Pelt.
Mr. George F. Wright.
   " Calvin E. Bush.
   " Oliver M. Bush.
   " Theodore T. Decker.
   " Dayton Decker.
   " John W. Decker.
   " Joseph S. Decker.
   " George W. Demarest.
   " Enos F. Depuy.
   " George B. Fancher.
   " James Grant.
   " John B. Hillyer.
   " William P. Hughes.
   " John N. Loblein.
   " Louis W. Lowe.
   " Wellington A. Merrell.
   " Elmer C. Merrell.
   " Eader Merrell.
   " William B. Minto.
   " W. Irving Morgan.
   " Frank Van Pelt.
   " Samuel W. Standring.
   " Thomas Lisk.

SUMMERFIELD M. E. CHURCH,

MARINERS' HARBOR, NEW YORK.

SUMMERFIELD M. E. CHURCH.

Mariner's Harbor.

CHAPTER XI.

SUMMERFIELD.

PREVIOUS to 1839, the Methodists living at Mariners' Harbor, Port Richmond and West New Brighton had no place of public worship nearer than New Springville, and those sturdy and devoted Christians were accustomed to walk miles over dark roads to attend not only the Sunday services but the week-day prayer-me tings as well. The neighbors would leave their small children in the care of one of their number while the parents and larger children made their nightly pilgrimages to their house of worship. [See reminiscences of the oldest Methodist on Staten Island—page 177].

From the time the old Neck (Asbury) church was built in 1802, until 1839—thirty-seven years—these people from all along the shore were accustomed weekly, and sometimes almost daily to travel the long distance to New Springville to church.

It is no wonder, therefore, that as soon as this portion of the congregation felt strong enough they should decide to build themselves a house of worship.

Accordingly, a meeting was held April 6th, 1839,

for the purpose of organizing a church, electing
trustees and taking measures to build a church on
or near the shore road at Mariners' Harbor.

At this meeting, Daniel Simonson, Benjamin B.
Kinsey, John L. Richards, Harry Jones and Peter
Braisted were elected trustees. At a meeting of
the board of trustees, held on the 30th of the same
month, it was resolved to call the new house, when
completed, "The Methodist Episcopal Church at
Mariners' Harbor." It was also resolved to borrow
$800, and commence the work of building immedi-
ately. The following day, May 1st, the board gave
the church note to Garrett Jones, Sr., for $800. On
the 4th of May, a certificate of the incorporation of
the Mariners' Harbor M. E. Church, was recorded
in the clerk's office of the county of Richmond,
signed by Daniel Simonson and John L. Richards.

A few days later, a lot, 130x60, on which to erect
this church, was purchased of Isaac Kruser, for
$275; and was conveyed to the trustees by deed
bearing date May 11th, 1839. On the 20th, a resolution was adopted, authorizing the board of trustees
to employ John L. Richards to superintend the
building of the church. The entire work on this
house was done by the day, and the whole cost was
about $2,000. The building was completed, and
neatly painted and furnished in November; and. on
the 1st of December, 1839, it was dedicated by the
Rev. Henry Chase, of the Mariners' Church, New
York city—the Revs. Daniel Parish, Mulford Day,
Henry Boehm and John S. Beegle taking part in the
services.

The Rev. Mulford Day, who had been on the
charge two years—1837-8—preached in the even-

ing. During the day, several propositions were made to raise the amount of indebtedness; but for want of concerted action, no pledges were obtained. This unfortunate circumstance led to much financial embarrassment during the first ten years of its existence. The following spring, 1840, the Island was divided, and is entered thus on the minutes of the New Jersey conference:

1840—Westfield, Daniel Parish.

1840—Northfield, Isaac Cross.

1841—Isaac Cross.

1841—Henry Boehm, supply.

The churches under the supervision of Isaac Cross were four in number—Asbury, Mariners' Harbor, Port Richmond and Quarantine. As soon as the church was dedicated, services were at once commenced, morning, afternoon and evening. As the preacher in charge, or his assistant, could only be present at one service, the pulpit was supplied by local preachers, among whom were the Revs. Elias Price and Inman Hall, of the Island, and the Rev. Messrs. Butler, McFarland, Sherwood and Curry, of New York. In the absence of ministers, the services were often conducted by Father Braisted, for many years a useful member of the Old Neck Church, and earnest exhorter, whose name occupies a prominent place in the annals of Methodism in this vicinity. During a part of this time Lewis R. Dunn, then a young man of much promise, was junior preacher.

In the spring of 1842, the Northfield charge was divided, and Robert Lutton was sent to Quarantine (Kingsley), and Port Richmond (Trinity), and Isaac N. Felch to Asbury and Mariners' Harbor. This year was one of prosperity. In the winter of 1842-3, a revival of religion took place at Mariners' Harbor, and many were added to the church. The following two years, George Hitchens was preacher in charge. During this period an effort was made by the pastor to pay off the church debt, which was still about $1,600. After several weeks of persevering effort, he succeeded in canceling one-half, leaving the remaining $800 unprovided for.

In the early part of 1845, the church was repainted and more tastefully fitted up, at a cost of less than $150. That year and the following, the Rev. W A. Wilmer was stationed preacher. In March 1847, to meet pressing liabilities, particularly interest on the church debt, a portion of the pews was rented, from which a small revenue was derived. This step was taken only after mature deliberation, and was the result of a majority vote of the male members of the church, at a meeting held January 25th, 1847. The years 1847-8 were years of prosperity for the society, under the pastoral care of the Rev. Abraham Owen. The year 1849 opened up a new era in the history of this society. This spring connection with the Neck was severed—Lewis R. Dunn being sent to that church, and the Rev. John Scarlett to Mariners' Harbor. In the spring of 1850, the Rev. Charles E. Hill was appointed to Port Richmond, with instructions to supply Mariners' Harbor till a young man could be provided as an assistant. In the autumn of that year there was one sent, who preached about four months with acceptability; but marked improprieties in his conduct were soon discovered, and he was summarily dismissed by the presiding elder of the district.

Through the intrigues of this person, dissensions sprang up in the church, and several of the members withdrew from its communion. But this event, which foreboded disaster to the temporal interests of Zion, was the very means used, under Providence, for attaining a higher state of prosperity, and hastened the final liquidation of a debt which had for so many years burdened the society. Under the pressure of circumstances, the leading men became responsible for sums ranging from $25 to $100 each; thus, in the easiest possible way, freeing the church of its liabilities. The last note for the largest of these sums was partly donated to the church, and on April 2nd, 1855, the original debt was officially reported paid. At that time, the church and its surroundings were also improved at a cost of about $200.

The Rev. C. E. Hill continued to fill the appointment till the conference of 1852, when the Rev. Benjamin Kelly was sent to Port Richmond, and also exercised control over the pulpit at Mariners' Harbor—preaching in the afternoon of each Sunday. In 1853, the Rev. Charles Miller was the pastor; and, toward the close of that year, fifty or sixty were hopefully converted, nearly all of whom at once united with the church. During this year the church was again repaired and painted, at a considerable cost. The Rev. S. T. Moore was preacher-in-charge for the years 1854-5.

At a special meeting of the board of trustees, held June 9th, in the last named year, a committee previously appointed reported that a parsonage had been purchased for $1,790. By a fortunate coincidence this house adjoins the lot where the new church was built. The church notes were immediately given to two parties, from whom the trustees had borrowed $1,400, with which to consummate the bargain. These were not entirely canceled till several years afterward (1861). The first church "fair and festival," on the charge, was held July 4th, 1855, and resulted in a clear profit of $456.

The Rev. C. A. Wombough was pastor during the years 1856-7, the Rev. John N. Crane in 1858-9. At this time morning preaching, which had been persevered in whenever practicable, under former pastors—particularly the Rev. J. Scarlett and the Rev. S. T. Moore—was resumed. The Rev. J. I. Morrow was the next preacher appointed, and served the church two years, 1860-1. In 1862-3, the Rev. H. A. Buttz was the stationed preacher. Toward the close of his term of service, the afternoon sermon was discontinued, and the morning session became much more important than in former years. In 1864-6, the Rev. George Winsor was the pastor. During the summer of 1864, the parsonage was repaired and enlarged, at an expense of $800. In 1867, the Rev. J. I. Morrow was appointed a second time to the charge, and remained three years. In the spring of 1867, the parsonage was again improved, at an expense of more than $300.

This brings us down to the period (1868) when the initial steps were taken in favor of erecting a new house of worship.

The following account of the erection of the "new church" is from the pen of the Rev. John I. Morrow, and was read at "the reunion meeting of former pastors," held in the church, Nov. 27th, 1870:

" It is well known that for years the want of enlarged and improved church accommodations had
been felt by the community. In the fall of 1868,
suggestions for the enlargement of the then exist-
ing house of worship were made, but negatived on
the ground of inexpediency. Proposals were next
made to build a new and more commodious house,
and for a time these were well nigh negatived, because of the supposed want of means. At length,
after several evenings' discussion of the subject, it
was resolved by the trustees to rise and build.

" Accordingly, plans and specifications were
adopted, and given to three parties as master builders, to estimate upon. Sealed proposals were handed in, and the contract awarded to Pero Brothers,
their estimate being much the lowest.

"On Thanksgiving day, the 26th of November,
1868, the contract was executed. This agreement
did not include the inside finish of the basement.
On the following 12th day of December, the corner-
stone of the edifice was laid with appropriate solem-
nities by the Rev. James Ayars, P. E. The Rev. J. N.
Crane conducted the opening exercises. The Rev.
M. E. Ellison addressed the audience, and made an
appeal for funds; when rising $600 were generously
contributed in money and pledges. Beneath the
stone was placed a box, suitably enclosed, containing the Bible, a Methodist hymn book, and discipline
of 1866, which were deposited as a memorial for future ages, that when the building, in the lapse of
time, shall have moldered into ruins, and the
stone be removed from its bed, generations to come
may thus learn the faith of those who were the
principal actors in this truly Christian enterprise.

" The box also contained copies of all the peri-
odicals and newspapers of the M. E. church in
the United States, also of the religious papers published weekly under the auspices of Methodism in
England and Canada; photographs of all the bishops
of the M. E. church; a sketch of the history of
Methodism in this community from 1839: a full list
of all the official and private members at that time
on the church records; a copy of the article of
agreement with the builders, and a list of subscriptions to build so far as obtained up to that time.

"On the 2nd day of March, 1869, the lot upon
which the church is built was enlarged by the purchase of an undivided half of the adjoining piece of
land, at a cost of $200. In June of this year, the so-
ciety held a meeting to grant the trustees power to
mortgage their church property to an amount not
exceeding $6,000, and also to change the name or title
of the church to Summerfield M. E. Church, all of
which power was granted the trustees by a unanimous vote. Shortly after this, the loan of $6,000
was effected, and then the trustees entered into a
second agreement with the builders for the inside
finish of the basement. The work went forward
until the building received its finishing stroke.

"On Sunday, Oct. 10th, 1869, at 10:30 o'clock a. m.,
the services of the dedication commenced.

" The order of the morning exercises were: Prayer,
by the Rev. James Ayars; reading the Scriptures,
by the Rev. J. N. Crane; sermon, by Bishop Janes,
on 2nd Corinthians, 6th chapter and 1st verse.

"At 3 p. m: Prayer, by the Rev. T. H. Smith;
sermon, by the Rev. M. E. Ellison.

"At 7 p. m.: Prayer, by the Rev. Mr. Harris, of

the Baptist Church; sermon, by the Rev. H. A. Buttz.

"The day proved stormy, and hence the faithful ones who were present had an excellent opportunity to taste how much better it is to give than to receive. The money and pledges obtained during the day amounted to about $2,000, which was not half the amount necessary to meet immediate claims. Here a crisis was reached. Although the new sanctuary had been entered, and we rejoiced in its occupancy, there remained yet to be expended a considerable sum in furnishing the basement with settees. Beside, much had to be done in the way of grading, flagging, and fencing the grounds of the building. Hence a meeting of the society was again called to empower the trustees to dispose of the old church property, and to effect, if possible, a second mortgage on the new church, to the amount of $2,000. The old church was accordingly sold for the sum of $1,500, and the loan of $2,000 made. Thus, by means of dedication moneys, the sale of the old church, and the second loan, all claims were promptly paid, and a small balance was left in the treasury. The entire cost of the church and its various fixtures was a fraction short of $24,000; and of this sum $16,000 were paid, leaving an encumbrance of $8,000 in two mortgages."

A few weeks after the dedication, the basement was furnished, and the Sunday-school occupied their new rooms. A want that had been long felt was now supplied, and the children seemed happy in view of their improved school accommodations. The next spring(1870), the Rev. Richard Harcourt received his appointment to this church, and in the autumn of that year, on the profession of their faith in Christ, sixty were received into the church on probation.

In 1871, the remaining half of the undivided lot mentioned above was secured on advantageous terms, and in the spring of 1872 another piece of land, adjoining and in the rear of the church and parsonage, was also bought and added to the property.

The old church is now the property of the W. C. T. U., but is used by the Salvation Army for their services.

In 1871, during the pastorate of the Rev. Richard Harcourt, the remaining half of the lot above mentioned was purchased, and the following spring the adjoining lot in the rear of the church and parsonage was secured, carrying the church property through the entire block.

In 1873, Mr. Harcourt was followed by the Rev. Thomas H. Smith who remained but one year, as the following year he was made presiding elder of the Newton district. During the year that he was pastor, $2,000 of the church debt was paid, reducing the amount from $8,000 to $6,000.

The next pastor was the Rev. A. M. Palmer, who remained three years. During his pastorate "ninety and nine" persons were received on probation.

The Rev. Cornelius Clarke, Jr., was appointed pastor in 1880. During his term, $2,000 were paid on the church debt, reducing it from $6,000 to $4,000, and 111 persons were received on probation.

In 1884, the second year of the pastorate of the Rev. John Krantz, Jr., now presiding elder of the Paterson district, the balance of the church indebtedness, $4,000, was paid and $1,700 additional were raised, and expended for repairs, principally in refurnishing and improving the lecture-room; the pastor's salary was increased from $1,100 to $1,500, and the collections for missionary and benevolent purposes were more than doubled. Eighty-six persons joined the church.

The Rev. Charles Larew, M. D., entered upon his duties as pastor of this church in 1886. During his term, a new roof was put on the church and other improvements made to the church and parsonage, costing in the aggregate about $500, and the church was lighted by gas.

In 1889, the Rev. W. S. McCowan, D. D., pastor, the Summerfield Church completed its first half-century of life and celebrated the event by the purchase of a pipe organ costing $1,700. This is a two-manuel full-pedal organ with 600 speaking pipes, manufactured by Odell Brothers, of New York. Of this amount $400 had already been raised and $1,100 were subscribed on "organ opening day."

The Rev. Dr. McCowan, in his history of Summerfield Church, gives the following account of the semi-centennial services:

"The semi-centennial of the Summerfield Methodist Episcopal Church, of Mariners' Harbor, Staten Island, was celebrated on Sunday, December 1st, 1889. The day was clear, and the church was crowded at all the services. The interior of the church was beautifully decorated with flags, shield and eagle, surmounted by a cross—appropriate emblems of religion and patriotism. A number of former pastors was present, namely: Revs. George Hitchens, Charles E. Hill, John N. Crane,

Henry A. Buttz, Thomas H. Smith, Abraham M. Palmer and C. Clark, Jr.

"The love-feast was held at 9 a. m., conducted by the Rev. A. L. Brice, D. D., presiding elder of the district. It was a long-to-be-remembered season of precious memories and spiritual power.

"At 10:30 a. m., the Rev. Henry A. Buttz, D. D., a former pastor, now president of Drew Theological Seminary, of Madison, N. J., preached a sermon of great sweetness and power, from 2 Thes., 1, 10.

"In the afternoon, at 2.30, the reunion service was held. The pastor, the Rev. W. S. McCowan, read a brief history of the church from its organization to the present time, and short addresses, full of pith and point, were made by Brothers Hitchens, Hill, Crane, Smith and Clark. Letters of congratulation were read from Brothers Morrow, Harcourt and Krantz, who, on account of previous engagements, were unable to be present.

"In the evening, at 7 o'clock, a praise service was held by the pastor. At 7:30, the Rev. A. M. Palmer, of the Newark conference, and a former pastor, preached an instructive sermon on the "Transfiguration of Christ," followed by an earnest exhortation by the Rev. C. Clark, Jr. The service closed with an old fashioned prayer-meeting.

"It was indeed a "red-letter" day in the history of Summerfield Methodist Episcopal Church—a day to which the people can ever point with honest pride, and to which, in years to come, her children can point with great satisfaction, that they were privileged to be present on an occasion so auspicious."

During the pastorate of Dr. McCowan, the church was favored with a great revival, during which 109 professed conversion, of whom 87 joined the church on probation.

In 1893, during the pastorate of the Rev. P. G. Blight, new carpets were purchased, the church was lighted by electricity, the parsonage repainted and the sidewalks in front of the church and parsonage flagged and curbed, the entire expenditure amounting to about $700.

In 1896, during the pastorate of the Rev. J. R. Bryan, D. D., the Sunday-school room was provided with new chairs and carpets, the walls were papered, the wood-work varnished, about $500 being spent in these and other improvements.

We are indebted to the "History of Summerfield Church" published by the Rev. Richard Harcourt and Mr. Theodore M. Decker in 1872, and the "Semi-Centennial History of Summerfield Church" published by the Rev. W. S. McCowan, D. D., in 1889, for much assistance in compiling the above history.

SUMMERFIELD'S PASTORS.

1839—Daniel Parish, died in Newark, N. J., April 1st, 1848, aged 48 years; 28 years in ministry.

1840-1—Isaac Cross, died in Washington, D. C., Nov. 21st, 1884, aged 73 years; 49 years in ministry.

1842—Isaac N. Felch, died at Hackettstown, N. J., March 24th, 1876, aged 69 years; 45 years in ministry.

1843-4—George Hitchens, died Aug. 27th, 1895, aged 80 years; 51 years in ministry.

1845-6—William A. Wilmer, died March 10th, 1878, aged 73 years; 31 years in ministry.

1847-8—Abraham Owen, died Aug. 1st, 1875, aged 75 years; 31 years in ministry.

1849—John Scarlett, died at Orange, N. J., Jan 18th, 1889, aged 86 years; 48 years in ministry.

1850-1—Charles E. Hill, superannuate, residence at Red Bank, N. J.

1852—Benjamin Kelly, died at Port Jervis, N. Y., Oct. 24th, 1874, aged 60 years; 32 years in ministry.

1853—Charles Miller.

1854-5—Samuel T. Moore.

1856-7—Cyrenius A. Wombough, died at Orange, N. J., Jan. 3rd, 1896, aged 70 years; 42 years in ministry.

1858-9—John N. Crane, died in Newark, N. J., July 9th, 1892, aged 81 years; 59 years in ministry.

1860-1—John I. Morrow, supernumerary, residence in Newark, N. J.; entered ministry in 1846.

1862-3—Henry A. Buttz, president of Drew Theological Seminary; entered ministry in 1858.

1864-6—George Winsor, died at Milford, Pa., Dec. 28th, 1884, aged 71 years; 45 years in ministry.

1867-9—John I. Morrow (see above).

1870-2—Richard R. Harcourt, stationed in Philadelphia, Pa.

1873—Thomas H. Smith, died at Wyoming, N. J., Aug. 4th, 1892, aged 72 years; 42 years in ministry.

1874-6—Abraham M. Palmer, supernumerary, residence in Newark, N. J.; entered ministry in 1842.

1877-9—Sylvester Opdyke, died at Newton, N. J., Oct. 21st, 1880, aged 53 years; 23 years in ministry.

1880-2—Cornelius Clark, supernumerary, residence at Dover, N. J.; entered ministry in 1857.

1883-5—John Krantz, presiding elder of the Paterson district; entered ministry in 1878.

1886-8—Charles Larew, supernumerary, residence at Mendham, N. J.; entered ministry in 1847.

1889-91—Winfield S. McCowan, stationed in Jersey City, N. J.; entered ministry in 1869.

1892-4—Peter G. Blight, stationed in Jersey City, N. J.; entered ministry in 1873.

1895-7—James R. Bryan, stationed at Somerville, N. J.; entered ministry in 1848.

1898—L. J. Johnston, present pastor; entered ministry in 1892.

PRESENT OFFICIALS.

TRUSTEES:

George T. Egbert, president; Uriah W. Osborne, secretary and treasurer; John S. Parker, Benjamin Van Pelt, John R. Tomlinson, John P. Kohler, John H. Post, Charles W. Decker, Paul V. Masters.

STEWARDS:

Abram E. Depuy, recording steward; Charles Houghwout, Robert Williams, Azel F. Merrell, Abram D. Jones, Edward P. Fox, David H. Osborne, George W. Miller, Nathaniel Moore, Ulysses G. Miller, Samuel Fisher, David B. Van Name, Paul V. Masters.

LADIES' AID SOCIETY:

The Ladies' Aid Society of this church was organized in 1894, with the following officers:

Mrs. John B. Kohler, president; Mrs. A. E. Depuy, vice-president; Mrs. D. B. Van Name, secretary; Mrs. George T. Egbert, treasurer.

The present officers are:

Mrs. W. J. Snyder, president; Mrs. Alfred Whiteley, first vice-president; Mrs. A. F. Merrell, second vice-president; Mrs. D. B. Van Name, secretary; Mrs. John Hann, assistant secretary; Mrs. George T. Egbert, treasurer.

KING'S DAUGHTERS:

This circle was organized in February 1890, and the officers chosen were:

Miss Mary Goss, president; Miss E. Ola Kinsey, vice-president; Miss Lizzie Miller, secretary; Miss Adilla Post, treasurer.

The present officers include:

Miss Addie Newman, president; Miss Gertrude De Hart, vice-president; Miss Ida Vaughn, treasurer; Miss Ida Jones, secretary.

SUNDAY-SCHOOL:

The Sunday-school was organized in May 1849. As no records are obtainable, except for the past few years, we are unable to give a correct list of the superintendents. The present officers are:

Azel F. Merrell, superintendent; Mrs. Ella Kinsey, assistant superintendent; George W. Egbert, secretary; Rudolph Merrell, treasurer; U. G. Miller, librarian; Herbert Osborne, assistant librarian; Miss Arberta Merrell, pianist.

CHRISTIAN ENDEAVOR SOCIETY:

This society was formed in September 1892, with 27 charter members, which number has been increased to 55. The first officers were as follows:

Rev. P. G. Blight, president; Miss Eugenia Jones, vice-president; George W. Miller, recording secretary; Miss Elizabeth Merrell, corresponding secretary; Miss Ida Wood, treasurer.

The last election resulted as follows:

Frank C. Merrell, president; Miss Addie A. Newman, vice-president; Rudolph Merrell, recording secretary; Miss Elizabeth Merrell, corresponding secretary; Robert F. Williams, Jr., treasurer.

JUNIOR CHRISTIAN ENDEAVOR:

The Junior Christian Endeavor Society was organized in January 1893, with 30 charter members. The first election resulted as follows:

Miss Priscilla Richmond, superintendent; Mrs. P G. Blight, assistant superintendent; Mrs. George T. Egbert, president; Miss Eugenia Jones, vice-president; Miss Lizzie Merrell, secretary; Miss Ella Newman, treasurer.

The present officers are:

Mrs. A. G. Kinsey, superintendent; Mrs. R. G. Marr, assistant superintendent; Miss Rena Marr, president; Miss Florence Besanko, secretary; Miss Adele Deming, treasurer; Miss Emma Decker, organist.

PRESENT MEMBERSHIP.

Mr. and Mrs. Elias Braisted.
    "   James Burtis.
    "   Hysen Burke.
    "   James A. Cole.
    "   Martin Christopher.
    "   Albert Christopher.
    "   Charles Brayne.
    "   John Brindley.
    "   George C. Calvert.
    "   Charles W. Decker.
    "   John B. Decker.
    "   Abram C. Depuy.
    "   Winfield S. Decker.
    "   Clarence DeHart.

Mr. and Mrs. Henry Fisher.
            "   Edward P. Fox.
            "   John W. Houseman.
            "   George T. Egbert.
            "   Abraham V. Jones.
            "   Abram D. Jones.
            "   Charles E. Hyde.
            "   John Henry.
            "   John Hann.
            "   William Merrell.
            "   Lafayette Merrell.
            "   Paul V. Masters.
            "   Nathan Moore, Sr.
            "   George W. Kinsey.
            "   George W. Miller.
            "   Nathan Moore, Jr.
            "   Azel F. Merrell.
            "   Freeman Merrell.
            "   Horace E. Morris.
            "   Henry Martineau.
            "   Clarence Miller.
            "   Charles W. Newman.
            "   David Osborn.
            "   Uriah Osborn.
            "   Garret D. Post.
            "   Ulysses G. Miller.
            "   Alonzo Merrell.
            "   Herman Richmond.
            "   Jos. M. Roberts.
            "   Clarence H. Sperry.
            "   John Post.
            "   William M. Pinder.
            "   Elmer Provost.
            "   David B. Van Name.

Mr. and Mrs. Franklyn Van Pelt.
"   Edward Slater.
"   John R. Tomlinson.
"   Alfred J. Whitely.
"   John Walbur.
"   Arthur Zeluff.
"   Charles Kruser.
"   George A. Post.
"   Bernard Van Name.
"   Albert P. Vroome.
"   Frank E. Vaughn.
"   Robert F. Williams.
Mrs. J. W. Snyder.
"   Ebenezer Elms.
"   Charles Decker.
"   Henry Kraeling.
"   Thomas J. Merrell.
"   Garrett B. Decker.
"   J. Parker Decker.
"   George Durrua.
"   Edgar Ellis.
"   Henry Fisher, Jr.
"   Henry De Hart.
"   Howard Decker.
"   Abraham Decker.
"   Samuel Collins.
"   J. Palmer Decker.
"   James Barron.
"   Robert Bailey.
"   David A. Barcalow.
"   Abraham Decker.
"   George S. Collins.
"   Winfield S. Kruser.
"   Clarence C. Conklin.

Mrs. William Cropper.
   " John Cannon.
   " David B. Barcalow.
   " Frank S. Burgess.
   " Moses B. Burbank.
   " William Hann.
   " William H. Houghwout.
   " Martin Houghwout.
   " Clarence Houghtaling.
   " George A. Henry.
   " Ella Kinsey.
   " William Houghwout.
   " A. D. Brown.
   " Augustus Heilman.
   " John S. Jones.
   " Isaac C. Moore.
   " Everett Martineau.
   " Matings S. Merrell.
   " John H. Merrell.
   " Robert Marr.
   " Charles W. Miller.
   " Samuel B. Van Nostrand.
   " Richard Williams.
   " Cedric S. T. Watson.
   " William Wright.
   " Budd Warthen.
   " William Wasson.
   " George Wallace.
   " Peter Van Name.
   " George Stinemire.
   " John B. Palmer.
   " Benedict Parker.
   " Harry Pettit.
   " David Pettit.

Mrs. George W. Schofield.
" William L. Stephens.
" John A. Snyder.
" H. J. Sharrett.
" Charles Strong.
" Henry P. Shotwell.
" George Thompson.
" Russell Tomlinson.
" Wesley Thompson.
" Garrett E. Van Pelt.
" O. N. Van Name.
" Jane Rustin.
" Mary T. Richmond.
" Ellen T. Squier.
" Charlotte Totten.
" Elizabeth J. Van Name.
" Sarah A. Morgan.
" Lizzie A. Miller.
" Sarah C. Neats.
" Charlotte E. Merrell.
" Rosena Vollmer.
" Theresa Van Nostrand.
" Ann E. Parker.
" Mary R. Burbank.
" Sarah Brink.
" Eliza T. Mersereau.
" Mary E. Huestess.
" Mary A. Kinsey.
" Abby W. Kinsey.
" Sarah Fisher.
" Sarah C. Doyle.
" Kate Decker.
" Nettie Ford.
" Hannah M. Gallis.

Mrs. Sarah C. Garthwaite.
" Catharine Decker.
" Phebe Jane Decker.
" Rebecca E. Decker.
" Ann De Hart.
" Frances Kruser.
" Ann Leonard.
" Aletta Latourette.
" Anna Leuthauser.
" Eliza Mersereau.
" Johanna Merrell.
" Adelia Morris.
" Annie Miller.
Miss Bertha Snyder.
" Annie Van Name.
" Mamie C. Vail.
" Lizzie Post.
" Elizabeth Jane Post.
" Bertha Post.
" Emily A. Rustin.
" Rodella Snyder.
" Ella Van Pelt.
" Lorena Wood.
" Ida Wood.
" Marion Miller.
" Edith Miller.
" Eva Miller.
" Minnie Miller.
" Evaline Martineau
" Blanche Merrell.
" Jennie Merrell.
" Addie Newman.
" Emily D. Osborn.
" Grace Osborn.

Miss Lizzie Merrell.
  "   Addie Merrell.
  "   Effie Markham.
  "   Arberta Merrell.
  "   Emma L. Marr.
  "   Nellie A. Marr.
  "   Ella Houghwout.
  "   Mamie Houghwout.
  "   Eugenia Jones.
  "   Ida Jones.
  "   Ella Jones.
  "   Sarah O. Jones.
  "   Florence Brink.
  "   Lavinia Brayne.
  "   Flora Blake.
  "   Ella M. Buffington.
  "   Lizzie E. Cannon.
  "   Mary Chapman.
  "   Laura Decker.
  "   Gertie De Hart.
  "   Carrie A. Decker.
  "   Emma Decker.
  "   Emma O. Cramer.
  "   Edith Decker.
  "   Alice M. Deming.
  "   Jennie Ellis.
  "   Addie Fisher.
  "   Albertina Fisher.
  "   Lottie Fisher.
  "   Mary E. Kinsey.
  "   Maggie Kneis.
  "   Bertha Kneis.
  "   Mabel Kinsey.
  "   Alice Latourette.

Miss Sarah Latourette.
    " Sadie Link.
Mr. Louis Latourette.
   " George Merrell.
   " George H. Kinsey.
   " George Kneis.
   " Henry Link.
   " Percy Egbert.
   " Samuel Fisher.
   " Charles Houghwout.
   " Clarence H. Decker.
   " George W. Egbert.
   " George W. Collins.
   " Henry M. De Hart.
   " Ellsworth Decker.
   " Nathaniel Barton.
   " Azel M. Burke.
   " Irwin Hyland.
   " Eugene Jones.
   " Samuel Jones.
   " Rudolph Merrell.
   " Frank Merrell.
   " Eurallis Merrell.
   " George E. Merrell.
   " Herbert Osborn.
   " Percy Osborn.
   " John S. Parker.
   " William B. Post.
   " William R. T. Marsh.
   " Samuel McCracken.
   " Thomas S. Merrell.
   " Ernest Miller.
   " Claude Martineau.
   " Oscar Merrell.

Mr. Charles Merrell.
  " Alfred Williams.
  " George Vaughn.
  " Nicholas Wright.
  " Robert Williams, Jr.
  " George J. Van Name.
  " Charles W. Richmond
  " Frank Snyder.
  " John H. Post.
  " Harry Perrine.
  " Frederick Parker.
  " Henry Tomlinson.
  " Drew Tomlinson.
  " Harry Totten.
  " Benjamin Van Pelt.
  " William Stephens, Jr.
  " Morton Slater.
  " Frank D. Sofield.
  " Louis Seawood.
  " John M. Tomlinson.
  " La Willa M. Cornelius.
  " Frederick Williams.

KINGSLEY M. E. CHURCH,

STAPLETON, NEW YORK.

KINGSLEY M. E. CHURCH.
Stapleton.

CHAPTER XII.

THE first meetings held by the Methodists at Stapleton were started by the Rev. Henry Boehm in the spring of 1835. These meetings were held for a time at the house of Mrs. White, corner of Cebra and St. Paul's avenues, and were near to the spot on which Kingsley Church now stands. St. Paul's avenue was then known by the suggestive name of Mud lane, and people who remember it in those days affirm that it lived up to its name.

Among those who attended these meetings and laid the foundations of Methodism in this part of the Island were Mrs. White, William Thorn, Mr. and Mrs. Kirby, Capt. and Mrs. Hart, William Howard and James White.

The attendance at these meetings increased rapidly, and it was soon necessary to provide larger quarters, and the services were transferred to the Academy.

Here, on the 12th and 19th of July, the Rev. Henry Boehm gave the first notice of steps to form a church, as follows :

"NOTICE.

" There will be a meeting of the members of the Methodist Episcopal Church on Staten Island on Tuesday, the twenty-first day of July next, at three o'clock in the afternoon, at the house of the Widow White at Tompkinsville, for the purpose of electing five trustees to erect and take in charge a meeting-house for the benefit of the Methodist Episcopal Church in the said village.

Dated, Staten Island, June 25th, 1835.

(Signed)   HENRY BOEHM,

Minister of the Circuit."

On July 22nd, the following articles of incorporation were filed in the county clerk's office at Richmond :

"WHEREAS, it being the intention of a number of the adult members of the Methodist Episcopal Church at Tompkinsville, on Staten Island, in the county of Richmond and state of New York, and elsewhere of the said county, to incorporate themselves into a religious society or congregation, pursuant to the statute in such case made and provided, the minister of the said church did publish for two successive Sabbaths, to wit : on the 12th and 19th days of July, 1835—being the days in which such church, congregation or society statedly met for public worship at the Academy in the said village—notice, of which the following is a copy :

" There will be a meeting of the members of the Methodist Episcopal Church on Staten Island on Tuesday, the 21st day of July next, at three o'clock in the afternoon, at the house of the Widow White at Tompkinsville, for the purpose of electing five

trustees to erect and take in charge a meeting-
house for the benefit of the Methodist Episcopal
Church in said village, dated, Staten Island, June
25th, 1835, and signed Henry Boehm, minister of the
circuit, at which time and place designated in the
said notice, to wit : on the 21st day of July, 1835,
at the house of the Widow White in the said village,
between the hours of three and five o'clock of that
day, the undersigned, William Cole and Jacob Braisted, were duly nominated and appointed by a majority of the members of the Methodist Episcopal
Church present to preside at the said election of
the said trustees and to receive the votes of the
electors and to be judges of the qualifications of
such electors, and the officers to return the names
of the persons who by a plurality of voies should
be elected to serve as trustees of the said church,
society or congregation;

"Now, therefore, we, the said William Cole and
Jacob Braisted, hereby certify that after we were
nominated as aforesaid we did preside at the elections which then and there took place for five trustees of the said society so to be formed, and that
we did receive the votes of the electors and did
judge of the qualifications, and that such election
did take place between the hours of three and five
o'clock in the afternoon of said day, and we further
certify that at such elections John Totten, Lawrence Hillyer, Henry Cole, Joseph Smith and Andrew C. Wheeler were duly elected trustees of the
said society, and that it was then and there determined by the electors aforesaid that the name and
title of the said trustees and their successors shall
forever be called and known and shall be the, In-

corporation of the Methodist Episcopal Church at Tompkinsville, Staten Island.'

" In witness whereof we, the inspectors aforesaid, have hereunto set our hands and seals this 21st day of July, 1835.

(Signed)   WILLIAM COLE.

JACOB BRAISTED."

The board of trustees met at Mrs. White's on July 21st and organized by electing Lawrence Hillyer, president ; Henry Cole, secretary, and Andrew C. Wheeler, treasurer.

Lawrence Hillyer, Joseph Smith and Andrew C. Wheeler were appointed a committee to apply for the money—$1,000--appropriated by the legislature for the building of the church.

Caleb T. Ward offered to give the trustees four lots on Cebra avenue, forming a plot one hundred feet square, as a site for a new church.

The next meeting of the board was held at the old Woodrow church, and the following resolutions were passed :

" *Resolved*, that whereas Caleb T. Ward, of Tompkinsville, has offered to give four lots of ground situated in said village, to the trustees for the purpose of erecting a place of worship thereon and to give us a deed in fee of the same,

" *Resolved*, that we accept the offer of Mr. Ward, and that Lawrence Hillyer and Joseph Smith be a committee to obtain a deed for the same.

" *Resolved*, that a committee be appointed to procure a plan for a church for the village of Tompkinsville and ascertain the probable cost of the same and report to the board at least by the 5th of March next, and that Joseph Smith, Lawrence Hillyer and Andrew Wheeler le that committee.

"*Resolved*, that the above committee prepare an application to the presiding bishop at the next Philadelphia conference for a missionary to be appointed to the Quarantine on this Island, and present the same through the presiding elder."

At a meeting of the trustees, held May 30th, 1837, Trustee Joseph Smith reported that he had received $1,000 from the state, and that it had been placed in the hands of the treasurer of the board of trustees.

At a meeting held June 13th, 1837, the following bids were received for erecting the church, 38x60 feet, according to plans prepared by Andrew D. Gale and adopted by the board : Lawrence Hillyer, $1,390 ; John H. Quilthot, $1,166 ; Andrew D. Gale, $1,225. James H. Quilthot, being the lowest bidder, received the contract, the church to be completed within three months.

Mr. Quilthot left the place before the building was completed, and, it is said, was never heard of afterward. The corner-stone was laid the 1st day of July, 1837, and the building was completed and dedicated about September 1st, 1838, and was fourteen months, instead of three months, in course of erection.

The vicinity of Widow White's house and the spot on which the church now stands was a cedar forest. The roads were only lanes, and in the spring of the year and after heavy rains were almost impassable. It was no uncommon thing to sink over shoe-top, and almost to the knees, sometimes when going to church.

When the first church was built there were but

three houses in all this section, viz.: Widow White's, Mr. Van Pelt's and the one opposite the German Church and owned by Mr. Van Buskirk. Afterward Mrs. Ward's was built, and the nearest was that built by Madam Grimes, a wealthy southern woman.

The Sunday-school was organized when the first church was opened in 1838, during the ministry of the Rev. Mulford Day, and William Thorn became the first superintendent. For fifteen years after the organization of the church it was connected with other Methodist churches on the Island on what is called the "circuit plan." The first pastor was the Rev. Henry Boehm. Father Boehm, as he was afterward called, lived to the advanced age of 100 years and died at Woodrow, December 28th, 1875.

The public services in the church were often conducted by local preachers in the absence of the pastors, and such names as Hall, Crain, Crawford, Howe and others are well remembered to this day.

The membership and congregation continued to increase, and the new church had not been in use many years before it was found necessary to provide a larger house. It was thought best also to secure a more convenient position. This movement first took definite shape in 1853. During that year the name of the church was changed to the Stapleton Methodist Episcopal Church, and arrangements were made to purchase a site from Richard Smith, on Richmond road and Beach street. The intention was to select some plan for the new church which would give opportunity to utilize the material in the old church, and after the old church was removed it was hoped that the four lots on which it stood could be sold and the amount turned in to the treasurer. Before the transaction was completed it was discovered that the old site, as soon as it ceased to be used for a Methodist Episcopal church, would revert to the grantor or his heirs. The trustees, therefore, found themselves in an embarrassing position. If they built on the lots contracted for they would lose the old site, and if they did not complete the purchase they would lose the $300 already paid. They appointed a committee to wait upon Mr. Smith and make the best terms with him that they could. He refused to refund the money paid, but stated that if the trustees would pay interest on the balance due he would give them time to sell the lots and save themselves from loss. But the final outcome was that the $300 were lost, and the new church was not built until two years later. On May 11th, 1855, the official board, consisting of the trustees, leaders and stewards, passed a resolution to build a new church, and appointed a committee, consisting of the pastor, the Rev. J. B. Graw, Messrs. Cisco, Willis, Morgan, Simpson and Kempton, to select plans, and on May 28th of that year the old church was sold at auction. Sidney N. Havens was the purchaser, and he removed it to New Brighton, where he remodeled it and fitted it up for a dwelling.

Plans for the new church were adopted May 21st, 1855, and in the following month the corner-stone of the second church building on this site was laid with suitable ceremonies. The church was dedicated in December of the same year.

During the interval from the sale of the old

church until the new building was completed, the services were held in the old Lyceum, for which the trustees paid rental at the rate of $100 per annum.

In 1853, the name of this church was changed to Stapleton Methodist Episcopal Church, and in 1857 it was changed to Cebra Avenue Methodist Episcopal Church.

During the ministry of the Rev. J. B. Faulks—1864-5—$1,500 of the church debt was paid, and during that of his successor, the Rev. John Coyle, the building was painted and papered and lighted by gas. $500 was expended during this time on improvements, all of which was paid.

In 1870, during the pastoral term of the Rev. Henry Spellmeyer, the church was raised and a basement was added to be used as a Sunday-school and lecture-room, and an extension of about 20 feet was built to the rear. These improvements, with the repainting and refurnishing which was done at this time, cost about $12,000. After these improvements its name was again changed, this time to Kingsley Methodist Episcopal Church, in memory of Calvin D. Kingsley of the M. E. church, who, while performing a tour of Episcopal visitation around the world, was attacked by disease and died at Beyroot, Syria, April 6th, 1870.

The building has a seating capacity of 500, and, with a commodious lecture-room for Sunday-school and social meetings, has abundance of room for carrying on the work. In 1878, Mr. Ward removed all restrictions on the title to the church site and gave the church a clear title in fee simple.

In 1879, $1,000 of the debt was paid, reducing the

amount to $3,000. The interest also was reduced from seven per cent. to six per cent.

At the second quarterly conference in 1883, at the suggestion of the pastor, the Rev. R B. Collins, a committee, consisting of S. N. Havens, William Buckner and James Ware, was appointed to inquire into the possibility of building a parsonage on the lot adjoining the church and donated by Mr. Ward, and to report at a subsequent meeting. Nothing was definitely decided upon until the first quarterly conference of 1884, when the matter was again brought up, and it was resolved to build a parsonage that year, and the president of the board of trustees was directed to call a meeting in furtherance of that object, and at the meeting so called it was decided to erect a parsonage on the lot, west of the church, to cost $3,000. The contract was awarded to Peter Post, and the building cost $2,995.20. Further items of expenditure brought the amount to about $3,500.

In January 1885, the Ladies' Parsonage Society was organized to furnish the parsonage. Mrs. Marion Vreeland was chosen president; Mrs. A. E. Braisted, vice-president; Miss Addie Morgan, secretary, and Mrs. G. P. Savacool, treasurer. The society held a fair in April and raised nearly $800.

In 1886, $1,400 was raised; the walls were kalsomined, the entire floor was carpeted, and new pews replaced the old ones. In 1887, jubilee services were held lasting one week, and with the money donated $700 of the debt on the parsonage was canceled and a grand Chickering piano purchased for the Sunday-school.

The following year the jubilee services of the

Sunday-school were held. A gracious revival began during the "week of prayer," and many of the young men of the community were converted.

In December 1890, the Young People's League, by a fair and other means, raised $400, with which the church and parsonage were painted and a new furnace procured.

In 1894, over $700 were spent in repairs and improvements. A new roof was put on the church at a cost of over $300; the improvements to the lecture-room, papering, carpeting, decorating, $364.70, and other repairs about $50.

In 1897, during the pastorate of the Rev. J. C. Howard, the Ladies' Mite Society was reorganized and the name changed to the Ladies' Aid Society. A prosperous Junior Epworth League was organized. A reading-room was opened, and new classes, to the number of seven, were formed.

In 1898, Kingsley has expended $250 in improvement of church auditorium, and $340 were added to the pipe-organ fund.

At the close of the conference year of 1897, a revival took place, which the presiding elder reported at the annual conference, as follows: "The revival in Kingsley Church was the best one known in its history. There were 80 accessions, including 57 on probation and 21 by letter and profession of faith."

In 1897-8, the benevolences exceeded any previous record of the church.

KINGSLEY'S PASTORS.

1837-8—Henry Boehm, died at Woodrow, N. Y., Dec. 28th, 1875, aged 100 years; 74 years in ministry.

1839-40—John S. Beegle, died at Millville, N. J.,
March 20th, 1882, aged 71 years; 41 years in
ministry.

1841—Isaac Cross, died in Washington, D. C., Nov.
21st, 1884, aged 73 years; 49 years in ministry.

1842—Robert Lutton, died Dec. 5th, 1858, aged 67
years; 21 years in ministry.

1843—Jefferson Lewis, died April 12th, 1895, aged
89 years; 51 years in ministry.

1844-6—Benjamin Day, died at Ann Arbor, Mich.,
Oct. 17th, 1891, aged 84 years; 59 years in ministry.

1847-8—George Winsor, died at Milford, Pa., Dec.
28th, 1884, aged 71 years; 45 years in ministry.

1849-50—Waters Burrows, died at Basking Ridge,
N. J., Mar. 4th, 1869, aged 79 years; 53 years in
ministry.

1851—B. D. Palmer.

1852—Supplied.

1853—John Stephenson.

1854—Charles Miller.

1855—Jacob B. Graw, stationed in Trenton.

1856—Dayton F. Reed, died at Flatbush, N. Y., Oct.
9th, 1860, aged 48 years; 10 years in ministry.

1857-8 (8 mos.)—H. S. Bishop.

1858 (4 mos.)—Elbert Clement, stationed at Ando-
ver, N. J.; entered ministry in 1860.

1858—W. H. Dickerson, died at Denville, N. J., Aug.
26th, 1880, aged 52 years; 26 years in ministry.

1859-60—A. S. Burdett.

1861—J. B. Stevens.

1862—Charles R. Snyder, died in Newark, N. J.,
Sept. 8th, 1895, aged 58 years; 34 years in ministry.

1863—Sylvester N. Bebout, stationed in Newark, N. J.; entered ministry in 1862.

1864-5—James B. Faulks, presiding elder Jersey City district; entered ministry in 1858.

1866 (6 mos.)—Theodore D. Frazee, stationed at Woodrow, N. Y.; entered ministry in 1862.

1866-8—J. Coyle, moved from conference, residence in California.

1869-71—Henry Spellmeyer, stationed at Roseville, N. J.; entered ministry in 1869.

1872—Jeremiah Cowins, died at Bound Brook, N. J., Feb. 3rd, 1897, aged 67 years; 41 years in ministry.

1873—George W. Smith, presiding elder Elizabeth district; entered ministry in 1873.

1874-5—H. M. Simpson, chaplain of Dr. Strong's Sanitarium at Saratoga, N. Y.; entered ministry in 1862.

1876—J. T. Michael.

1877-8—J. F. Andrew, stationed at Paterson, N. J.; entered ministry in 1876.

1879-81—Charles S. Woodruff, stationed at Dover, N. J.; entered ministry in 1871.

1882—Charles W. McCormick, stationed at Hackettstown, N. J.; entered ministry in 1881.

1883-5—Robert B. Collins, stationed at Tottenville, N. Y.; entered ministry in 1863.

1886-90—J. G. Johnston, stationed at Bloomfield, N. J.; entered ministry in 1877.

1891-3— S. N. Bebout. (See above.)

1894-6—F. A. Mason, stationed at Franklin, N. J.; entered ministry in 1867.

1897—James C. Howard, present pastor; entered ministry in 1887.

PRESENT OFFICIALS.

TRUSTEES:

John Carmichael, vice-president; H. G. Simpson, treasurer; George Ware, secretary; Leander Cubberly, John Van Nostrand.

The office of president is vacant, owing to the recent death of this trustee.

STEWARDS:

J. J. Wood, William Irving, William B. Merritt, George L. Egbert, F. R. Harreus, Stanley B. Patrick, William MacDonald, George Clapp.

STEWARDESSES:

Mrs. Rebecca Ludlum, Mrs. Hester Morgan, Mrs. Mary J. C. Howard, Mrs. Hannah Brown, Miss Sarah W. Ludlum, Mrs. Carrie G. Post.

LEADERS:

H. G. Simpson, John McDowell, James Brown, Leander Cubberly, William Woelfle.

Local preacher: John A. Aspinwall.

SUNDAY-SCHOOL :

D. I. Aspinwall, superintendent; William Johnson, assistant superintendent; B. F. Stanton, second assistant superintendent; Miss Rebecca Ludlum, secretary and treasurer; F. R. Harreus, librarian ; Miss A. B. Morgan, pianist.

EPWORTH LEAGUE :

Kingsley Epworth League was formed Sept. 20th, 1892, and has a membership of 75. The first officers were as follows :

Thomas Bynner, president ; Miss Minnie Bebout, secretary ; Miss Lou Bebout, treasurer.

The present officers are as follows :

F. H. Harreus, president ; Mrs. James E. Brown, first vice-president ; Miss Sarah W. Ludlum, second vice-president : William B. Merritt, third vice-president : Mrs. Charles T. Wood, fourth vice-president : William MacDonald, secretary : Miss Emma A. Ludlum, treasurer.

JUNIOR EPWORTH LEAGUE :

Kingsley Junior Epworth League was organized June 5th, 1897, and has a membership of 75. The officers elected are :

Miss Hattie Morecock, president : Miss Annie Deible, vice-president ; Roy Howard, financial secretary ; Robert Simpson, corresponding secretary ; Miss Edith Savacool, secretary : Miss Grace Redmond, treasurer ; Mrs. Hannah Brown, superintendent : Miss Sarah Ludlum, superintendent mercy and help department.

PRESENT MEMBERSHIP.

Mr. and Mrs. William Andrews.
"   George W. Alston.
"   James E. Brown.
"   George Clapp.
"   George L. Egbert.
"   John G. Fence.
"   William T. Hagadorn.
"   F. R. Harreus.
"   William Irving.
"   William E. Johnson.
"   Harrison Johnson.
"   William Mac Donald.
"   John MacDowell.
"   William B. Merritt.
"   John Moore.
"   George P. Savacool.
"   Henry G. Simpson.
"   Alexander Trumpore

Mr. and Mrs. William H. Tong.
    "   John Van Nostrand.
    "   Charles T. Wood.
    "   George Ware.
    "   James Ware.
    "   John J. Wood.
    "   Daniel Wandell.
    "   Samuel McDowell.
    "   Stanley B. Patrick.
Mrs. William J. Burbank.
  " David M. Barrow.
  " Abraham Braisted.
  " Thomas Gordon.
  " Samuel Gordon.
  " William Haines.
  " William Ludlum.
  " Joseph Nelson.
  " Samuel Pritchett.
  " Frederick Spender.
  " Frank Van Pelt.
  " Levi Van Nostrand.
  " James P. White.
  " William Shephard.
  " William Trumpore.
  " Samuel Trumpore.
  " Charles Blake.
  " Charles Wood.
  " Wiiliam Bennett.
  " George Everson.
  " Lilian Kelsey.
  " Mary Schwab.
  " Sarah Meldowney.
  " Elizabeth Oberg.
  " Carrie G. Post.

Mrs. Mary J. Reckbow.
  " Catherine Sherding.
  " Jennie Sharrott.
  " Addie St. John.
  " Anna J. Taxter.
  " Maria J. Van Cott.
  " Mary Ware.
  " Eliza Flynn.
  " A. C. Morecock.
  " Jane Balsover.
  " Christina Poock.
  " A. E. Campbell.
  " Mary Clayton.
  " Amelia Blake.
  " Elizabeth Bush.
  " Mary E. Brown.
  " Hannah Crossley.
  " Elizabeth Fink.
    Arabella Havens.
  " Eliza Hetherington.
  " Mary M. Hamilton.
  " L. Heyne.
  " Annie Ingle.
  " Eliza J. Morgan.
Miss B. M. Holsapple.
  " Tillie Aspinwall.
  " Maud Aspinwall.
  " Ida May Blackburn.
  " Miss Emilia A. Balch.
  " Maria G. Balch.
  " Sue L. Barrow.
  " Annie E. Davis.
  " Jennie Gordon.
  " Emily Gordon.

Miss Eliza Griffith.
    " Salina Griffith.
    " Emma Harreus.
    " Christiana Johnson.
    " Edna Jones.
    " Emma A. Ludlum.
    " Sarah W. Ludlum.
    " Rebecca M. Ludlum.
    " Addie B. Morgan.
    " Hester J. Morgan.
    " Almira D. Ludlum.
    " Mary W. Mason,
    " Hattie Fink,
    " Susie Ludlum,
    " Martha Moore.
    " Laura Sherding.
    " Hattie Sherding.
    " Lucy Wandell.
      Mary Elizabeth Williams.
    " Ella Yerks.
    " Hattie Morecock.
    " Annie E. McIntyre.
    " E. M. Hagemann.
Mr. Jesse D. Moseley.
    " Theodore Brower.
    " Frank Deibel.
    " Archie McDowell.
    " Martin Harris.
    " Charles S. Trumpore.
    " William Woelfle.
    " Samuel M. White.
    " James Buckley Willis.
    " David Van Pelt.
    " Fred. T. Tong.

Mr. John Tong.
"   Joshua Tushingham.
"   Fred Schwartz.
"   George Richardson.
"   George Richardson, Jr.
"   William W. Osborn.
"   Elijah Nichols.
"   William E. Knight.
"   C. W. Johnson.
"   Frank M. Harrington.
"   John Carmichael.
"   Leander Cubberly.
"   Abram Braisted.
"   Thomas H. Bynner.
"   John Aspinwall.
"   Eddie Aspinwall.

TRINITY M. E. CHURCH,

WEST NEW BRIGHTON, NEW YORK.

TRINITY M. E. CHURCH.
West New Brighton.

THE formative period of the Port Richmond church (now Trinity Methodist Episcopal Church), as distinct from Asbury, embraces the years of 1838 to 1839, the Methodists of Port Richmond and its vicinity having accepted the offer of Robert C. Simonson to give them a lot, upon condition of their building there-on.

He conveyed it to them Dec. 1st, 1839, and the church on Pond road (now Jewett avenue) was dedicated early in the winter of 1839. It is said that the Methodists of Port Richmond and Mariners' Harbor contemplated erecting a building in the vicinity of Graniteville for their joint occupation. But, disagreeing in this contemplated project, they separated like Abram and Lot, or rather like two sisters, each determining to set up for herself.

This sisterly feeling seems to have continued in later years, for when both had determined to hold festivals the same evening, Trinity yielded, deeming it improper that they should conflict with each other.

The deed of the Harbor church bears the date of

May 11th, 1839, and on the first day of December 1839, the church was dedicated.

At this time the charge included Asbury and Mariners' Harbor. In 1842, Asbury and Mariners' Harbor were set apart as a separate charge.

In 1840, Staten Island station reported 432 members; Quarantine reported 24 members. At this conference a new division of the territory took place—a Westfield and a Northfield charge. The Rev. Daniel Parish was appointed to Westfield, and the Rev. Isaac Cross to Northfield and Quarantine mis_ sion. In 1841, Mr. Cross was appointed to Northfield, and in 1842 the charge reported 400 members At this conference, Northfield was divided into Northfield charge, embracing Asbury and the Harbor churches, and the new charge called Quarantine and Port Richmond, to which the Rev. R. Lutton was sent as pastor. This change severed the connection of Port Richmond and the Neck, now known as Asbury, for though they had had their own house of worship for four years, they had continued their con_ nection with the mother church. Thus the Port Richmond, now Trinity, church may be considered the great-granddaughter of old Woodrow.

At this date, May 16th, 1842, we have the earliest record of this organization. It is found in the book containing the proceedings of the first quarterly conference of the Quarantine and Port Richmond charge, held at Port Richmond. There were present the Revs. W. Burrows, R. Lutton, Inman Hall, John B. Hall, G. H. Houghwout, Wm. M. Thompson, Wm. D. Simonson, J. A. Thompson and Isaac N. Brown. These men were also appointed stewards.

At this conference, the committee appointed to

estimate the expenses for the year reported the amount necessary, $541.50.

Although Quarantine holds the first place in the name of the charge, we find that three out of four quarterly conferences were held at Port Richmond this year.

In 1843, the Quarantine and Port Richmond charge reported 152 members. At this conference Staten Island was made a charge of Rahway district and the Rev. R. Lutton was re-appointed pastor.

The charge reported 138 members in 1846, a decrease of 14, probably owing to the enforcement of discipline.

In 1848-9, the Rev. Alexander Gilmore was the preacher in charge of the North side. The minutes say this church was not connected with Quarantine these years. Doubtless there were other preaching places, perhaps at New Brighton, as there was preaching there in 1854, when it was resolved to discontinue it in deference to the wishes of the Quarantine brethren.

In 1850-1, the Rev. Charles E. Hill was appointed to the Port Richmond charge, with instructions to supply Mariners' Harbor until a young man could be procured as an assistant.

In 1852, Port Richmond and Mariners' Harbor were regularly united in one charge. In the minutes of this year we have the first report of membership of Port Richmond There were 112 members and 4 probationers and of Mariners' Harbor, 57 members.

In 1853, Port Richmond became a separate charge, taking the name of Trinity Methodist Episcopal Church, Castleton, with the Rev. B. Kelly as pastor.

This is an important epoch in the church life. The church had reached her majority and become independent, not only of her mother, but also of her sister. A brief history of this new departure and grand enterprise of building a new church edifice must now be given.

The first intimation of building a new church occurs in the minutes of the quarterly conference, held Jan. 27th, 1851, under the pastorate of the Rev. C. E. Hill:

"WHEREAS, the male members of this society held a meeting on the 13th of July to consider the expediency of erecting a new house of worship, and did at that meeting adopt resolutions expressive of the wants of the society, and appointed a committee to consider plans, costs, etc , therefore be it resolved that their action be confirmed."

J. W. Snedeker, J. G. Cadmus, L. Edwards, John Q. Simonson, Samuel Thompson and Capt. D. Latourette were appointed a building committee to erect a new house of worship on the lot between Factoryville and Port Richmond. The church had previously purchased the lot for $525. The assets of the church at this date were $1,368. At the quarterly conference held Dec. 25th, 1862, the following action was taken:

"WHEREAS, it appears that the organization of our church as it now is, is illegal and in a meas ure void, according to the revised statutes of this state, etc.

Resolved, in the quarterly conference assembled, that the present board of trustees, together with the pastor, be and is directed forthwith, to call a meeting of the male members of the society for the purpose of electing a board of trustees in accordance with the laws of the state."

Notice was duly given Dec. 26th. The election took place Jan. 10th, 1853. Lewis Edwards, J. G. Cadmus, John Q. Simonson, Azariah Dunham, and J. W. Snedeker were elected. The board organized by electing J. W. Snedeker president. It was resolved at the same time that the newly elected board assume the name and title of trustees of the Trinity Methodist Episcopal Church, Castleton, Staten Island.

A copy of the proceedings of the meeting was sent to the county clerk to be recorded. On account of the destruction by fire of the records made previous to June 28th, 1854, we have no account of the further action in connection with the building of the church.

It is doubtful whether the original building committee, appointed Jan. 27th, 1851, acted in building the present edifice; at least, we have no report of any action.

On Feb. 9th, 1852, J. G. Cadmus was appointed to see if a sufficient sum could be obtained to build a parsonage. We find no report of the action of this representative, but it is probable that the report was favorable, as the parsonage was soon built.

Trinity Methodist Episcopal Church was dedicated Jan. 29th, 1853. According to the treasurer's report of Jan. 8th, 1855, the total amount of cash paid for building the church was $9,192.42, and total indebtedness was $5,205.13.

In 1854, a proposition was received from the German Lutheran Evangelical Society for the purchase of the North side (Port Richmond Methodist Episcopal Church) for $1,500. Of this sum, $1,000 were to be collected and paid by G. P. Dissosway. The proposition was accepted. Of the circumstance of dedication we find no account. Bishop Janes, the Rev. R. S. Foster, now bishop, and the Rev. J. B. Makley were advertised in the *Christian Advocate* to take part in the services, also the Revs. J. K. Shaw, C. H. Whitaker and George Hughes were announced to participate in the services on the following Sunday. The following were the members of the board at the time of dedication: J. G. Cadmus, J. W. Snedeker and L. Edwards were trustees, stewards and leaders; Wm. Greer was leader, J. Q. Simonson, R. T. Jones and A. Boyce were stewards. These were present at the first quarterly conference, held for the new charge, Jan. 25th, 1853.

At the time of dedication the membership was 112, as nearly as we can make out. The pastor reported the number of scholars in the Sunday-school as 125, officers and teachers 21, and the school constantly increasing in number and interest.

In 1854, the school reports 190 scholars on the roll and 25 officers and teachers, with an average of 130 scholars and 21 teachers. The pastor's report was, "The school is in active, prosperous and useful existence."

In the year ending with the spring of 1853, the total expenses, exclusive of those of the trustees for both Port Richmond and Mariners' Harbor, amounted to $683. In 1853-4, the first year of the new church, the total amount contributed for the same purpose was $1,238, or nearly double that of the previous year. This shows that a remarkable impulse had been given to the cause of God by the completion of the new enterprise.

The Rev. T. Pearson succeeded Mr. Kelly and was pastor in 1854-5. The spirit of Catholicity seems to have prevailed in those early times, for we find the following minutes in the stewards' records under the date of Oct. 8th, 1855: "On motion it was voted to invite the congregation of the Rev. Mr. Brownley, the Rev. Mr. Sage and the Rev. Mr. White to unite with us in our religious services on Thanksgiving day, and that the Rev. Mr. Brownley be invited to preach on that occasion."

In 1855, the church was made a separate charge and took the name of Trinity. The Rev. Benjamin Kelly was the first pastor.

Under later date we find the following in the minutes: "It was requested that it be recorded that the Thanksgiving service be as agreed upon."

This was probably the first union Thanksgiving service held by the churches of Port Richmond and West Brighton. The Rev. N. Vansant was appointed to the charge for the years of 1856-7. During the last year there was a remarkable revival, the largest ever enjoyed by the church. Mr. Vansant reported 115 probationers, and many in the church now were received at that time, and have served faithfully all these years.

The Rev. M. E. Ellison came after Mr. Vansant in 1858. His pastoral fidelity saved a large number of probationers left to his care. The Rev. J. M. Freeman filled the station in 1860 and 1861.

He was succeeded by the Rev. R. S. Arndt, who remained two years. In 1864, the Rev. J. O. Winner was appointed, remaining but one year. During his term, Jan. 16th, 1865, a resolution to pay the church debt was made;

"*Resolved*, that we deem it expedient to liquidate the church debt, in shares of $10 each."

Mr. Arndt was succeeded by the Rev. J. E. Hurst, who was removed in the second year and appointed to missionary work in Germany. He had a good revival. The Rev. N. Owen was appointed to fill out Dr. Hurst's second year. It was during his short pastorate that difficulties which had been growing for a year or two past culminated in a secession and in the formation of a new organization at Port Richmond. We are unable to give the number of those who went out from the old church as the record does not show. They either removed by certificate or withdrew. In 1866, just before the trouble, the minutes give a membership of 249 and 79 probationers. Of these probationers 33 only were received. This would give a total of 282 members, but the minutes of 1877 gave a membership of 205, the difference being 76. "The History of Staten Island" states that on Jan. 23rd, 1867, 48 persons, most of them seceders from Trinity Methodist Episcopal Church, Port Richmond, were then and there constituted into a new church by the presiding elder to be called the "North Shore Free Methodist Episcopal Church."

In 1867, there were 24 probationers, though no new ones for that year. They were probably part of the 40 received in 1866. Thus this number was reported twice. This may answer the question, what becomes of our probationers? The wholesale backsliding from 1866 to 1867 doubtless was largely owing to the bitter feeling which prevailed at that time, resulting in a division, and continuing after it.

The church records give very little about the un-

happy affair.   Just after the annual election of the
trustees on Jan. 7th, 1867, four members of the
board offered their resignations, which were accepted
Jan. 14th, 1867. On Feb. 18th, their places were filled
by Samuel Loveland, Howard Miller, Wm. D. Simonson and Captain Anderson.   After this everything
went on in peace and harmony.   The next pastor
was the Rev. T. H. Smith, who is the only preacher
that remained three years.   These were three years
of great prosperity.   In 1867, a resolution was made
to pay off the church debt, each member to give what
he could, and the pastor to endeavor to secure the
services of one of the prominent bishops to help
forward the work.

The effort was successful, for we find that in July
$1,875 were pledged. The pastor headed the list with
$50 and a layman subscribed $800. By September
the amount had reached $2,488.

In 1868, the church was painted and papered and.
the grounds improved, at a cost of $737.   The organ
was purchased this year, and the majority of the
board of trustees thought that the prelude should
be short and the interlude dispensed with.   But
after ten years, on May 20th, 1872, the consent of
the trustees was given to the choir to obtain a large
organ, without any restrictions as to interlude.

On June 22nd, a resolution was passed to complete
the tower.   The lowest estimate on it was $2,500,
which makes the cost of the church $12,164.

June 10th, 1870, another proposition was made to
pay the debt of the church, and a subscription was
opened.   Mr. Stothers subscribed $100 and another
member $150. The debt in 1855 was $5,205, most of
which was carried sixteen years.   There was not

much progress in paying it off until the Rev. Mr. Hurlbert's pastorate in 1872. The treasurer reported that there had been received on account of the church debt $4,560, paid out on same $4,602, leaving a deficiency of $42.70. This was certainly a triumph" ant struggle with an embarrassing burden.

This sketch would be incomplete without a few remarks about the Sunday-school.

The reorganization of the Sunday-school took place in February 1853 by the adoption of a proper constitution and the election of officers. J. G. Cadmus was elected superintendent and Charles N. Snedeker secretary and treasurer.

Just before the dedication of the new church twenty-five years before, it was resolved to procure a suitable banner for the Sunday-school, and also badges. On the morning of the dedication the of- ficers, teachers and scholars assembled in the old church, and after having their badges put on and singing a parting hymn of praise on leaving their old home, at the appointed hour, passed two by two into the new house of worship, preceded by the banner; The scene was witnessed with delight by all who beheld it. The first session was held in the new church on Sunday morning, July 3rd. The school occupied the gallery, as the lecture-room was not finished. It prospered greatly, and the pastor's report shows that it about doubled in the first four months.

In April 1882, the Rev. G. W. Smith was appointed pastor of the Trinity charge. On reaching his appointment he was impressed with the fact that the church was in a very bad condition, both inside and outside. In September, he asked the board of

trustees to hold and appoint a committee to examine the church, and make recommendations to
the board. This was done and E. D. Clark, W. H
Lyons and D. H. Houghwout were appointed with
the pastor as a committee. After examination they
informed the board that the necessary improve
ments would cost $1,700. The trustees thought
this sum would be almost impossible to raise, and
the church would be put in debt, but the pastor
thought otherwise, and asked their permission to
go among the people and see if from their gener-
osity it could not be raised. After two weeks he
called a meeting of the board and informed them
that he had raised $1,530. The committee then
went heartily into the work of making improvements, which cost altogether $2,998.

The church was completed and re-opened on Dec.
24th, 1882.

The parsonage was built in 1887 and cost about
$6,000. It is one of the finest parsonages on the
Island. In 1890, the front of the church was covered with a coating of cement to improve its general appearance, but the work proved a failure as
the cement cleaved loose and large pieces fell ex-
posing the brick, giving the front a very unpleasing
appearance.

The church was first lighted by electricity in
1892, new chandeliers and carpets were purchased,
and improvements made to the parsonage, costing
altogether about $800.

Recently, an entire new front of buff-colored, rock-
faced brick has been built, the side walls have been
painted to match the front in color, a new roof put
on the church and other improvements, which,

when finished, will have cost about $3,500.

During the past ten years, this congregation have spent a large amount of money on their church and parsonage, and now have a property of which they may well feel proud, and they may reasonably hope to be exempt from any large expenditures for a long time.

We are unable to give a list of the members, as the pastor and official board object to the names being published This is the only reason why a solitary exception is made in the case of this church.

LIST OF PASTORS.

1840-1—Isaac Cross, died in Washington, D. C., Nov. 21st, 1884, aged 73 years ; 49 years in ministry.

1843—Robert Lutton, died Dec. 5th, 1858, aged 67 years ; 21 years in ministry.

1842—Robert Lutton.

1844—George Hitchens, died Aug. 27th, 1895, aged 80 years ; 51 years in ministry.

1845-6—Wm. A. Wilmer, died March 10th, 1878, aged 73 years ; 31 years in ministry.

1847—Jefferson Lewis.

1848-9—Alexander Gilmore, died Jan. 28th, 1894, aged 82 years ; 57 years in ministry.

1850-1—Charles E. Hill, superannate, residence at Red Bank, N. J.

1852-3—Benjamin Kelly, died at Port Jervis, N. Y., Oct. 24th, 1875, aged 60 years ; 32 years in ministry.

1854-5—Thomas W. Pearson, died at New Providence, N. J., May 28th, 1860, aged 56 years ; 35 years in ministry.

1856-7—Nicholas Vansant, supernumerary, residence at Madison, N. J.; entered ministry in 1842.

1858-9—M. E. Ellison, died in Jersey City, N. J., March 6th, 1882, aged 64 years; 39 years in ministry.

1860-1—J. M. Freeman, assistant editor Sunday-school and Tract Publication, New York.

1862-3—Ralph S. Arndt, died in Newark, N. J., Aug. 17th, 1892, aged 66 years; 43 years in ministry

1864—J. O. Winner, stationed at Verona, N. J.; entered ministry in 1887.

1865-6—John F. Hurst, ordained bishop in 1880; residence in Washington, D. C.

1867-9—Thomas H. Smith, died at Wyoming, N. J., Aug. 4th, 1892, aged 72 years; 42 years in ministry.

1870-1—James O. Rogers, died at Hackensack, N. J., April 11th, 1887, aged 74 years; 51 years in ministry.

1872-3—J. Lyman Hurlbut, corresponding secretary of the Sunday-school Union and Tract Society of the M. E. church.

1874-5—John B. Taylor, stationed at Montville, N. J. entered ministry in 1865.

1876-8—Solomon Parsons, died at Paterson, N. J Nov. 21st, 1897, aged 65 years; 39 years in ministry.

1879-81—Nicholas Vansant, supernumerary, residence at Madison, N. J.; entered ministry in 1842.

1882-3—George W. Smith, presiding elder Elizabeth district; entered ministry in 1873.

1884—Lewis R. Dunn, superannuate, residence at East Orange, N. J.; entered ministry in 1841.

1885-7—Samuel P. Hammond, presiding elder Newark district; entered ministry in 1871.
1888—John Crawford, died at Rome, N. Y., July 7th,
1897, aged 47 years; 21 years in ministry.
1889-93—D. B. F. Randolph, stationed in Jersey
City, N. J.; entered ministry in 1871.
1894-6—William B. Wigg, supernumerary, residence
at Paterson, N. J.; entered ministry in 1865.
1897—Enoch Meacham, present pastor; entered
ministry in 1874.

PRESENT OFFICIALS.

TRUSTEES :

E. D. Clark, president; D. Stothers, secretary;
J. A. Hillyer, treasurer; Wm. H. Lyons, George
P. Rowe, A. C. Gibson, A. C. Hillyer, C. W. Kennedy,
David T. Houghwout.

STEWARDS :

Benedict Parker, Otis Kennedy, Ephraim Smith,
George Kelley, F. F. Norton, George Smith, George
Pero, J. W. Bodine, E. C. Layman, E. W. Durkin,
A. E. Gibson, A. C. Hillyer, Elmer H. Simonson.

SUNDAY-SCHOOL :

James A. Hillyer, superintendent; Mrs. S. M.
Morris, assistant superintendent; Elmer H. Si-
monson, secretary; Miss Ella Parker, treasurer;
Miss Emma Berry, librarian.

CHRISTIAN ENDEAVOR :

The society of Christian Endeavor was organized
Jan. 10th, 1889, with a charter membership of 17.
This number has been increased to 45.

The first officers were: Miss Florence D. Hunes,
president; Alfred Gibson, vice-president; Rush
Robinson, recording secretary; Miss Bertha Sur-

dam, corresponding secretary ; Miss Kate Kennedy, treasurer.

The present officers are : Miss Winnie Sterns, president ; Thomas Stinemire, first vice-president ; Miss Martha Murray, second vice-president ; Miss Ellie Parker, corresponding secretary ; Miss Adele Taylor, recording secretary ; E. H. Simonson, treasurer.

LADIES' AID SOCIETY :

This society was formed June 24th, 1867. The membership numbers 91. Those who served as first officers were : Rev. Thomas H. Smith, president ; Mrs. William Snedeker, directress ; Mrs. H. R. Miller, secretary ; Mrs. Matilda Smith, assistant secretary ; Mrs. James Hillyer, treasurer.

At present the officers consist of the following : Rev. Enoch Meacham, president ; Mrs. Matilda Hallock, directress ; Mrs. Lewis Simonson, secretary ; Mrs. A. C. Hillyer, treasurer.

JUNIOR CHRISTIAN ENDEAVOR :

Trinity Junior Christian Endeavor was organized Oct. 30th, 1892, with 30 members and the following officers :

Miss Kate Brewster, president ; Arthur Taylor, vice-president ; Miss Nettie Galer, recording secretary ; Miss Carrie Pickens, treasurer.

The present officers are : Lewis Hillyer, president ; Miss Gertrude Chappelle, vice-president ; Miss Nellie Blake, recording secretary ; Miss Edna Pine, treasurer.

.

GRACE M. E. CHURCH.

PORT RICHMOND, NEW YORK.

GRACE M. E. CHURCH.
Port Richmond.

CHAPTER XIV.

GRACE METHODIST EPISCOPAL CHURCH at Port Richmond is the offspring of Trinity M. E. Church at West New Bright

During the pastorate of the Rev. Abraham Owen, difficulties which had been growing for some time, culminated with the withdrawal of a large number of members, who determined in the interest of harmony to secede and form the separate organization.

On January 10th, 1867, a meeting was held at the house of Read Benedict to decide what measures they would take in order to secede from Trinity Church.

The following are the names of the people who met and drew up the resolutions:

Frank G. Johnson, Ward McLean, Wm. Greer, N. P. H. Barrett, John Q. Simonson, Japhet Alston, Sedate M. Turner, R. P. Brown, George F. Heal, Wm. H. Perry, Isaac W. Fuller, Phillip H. Rustin, Horace F. Barrett, Thomas Taylor, Mathew Taylor, Wm. Simonson, Joseph Simonson, Mulford D. Simonson, Jasper G. Cadmus, Elias Baldwin, John S. Sprague.

The following resolutions were drawn up:

"Herein the undersigned pledge ourselves to each other to unite the formation of a society to be known as the North Shore Free Methodist Episcopal Church of Staten Island. To sustain the same, we pledge our constant prayer and our best efforts and influence, and our means in the proportions that God has given us, and we hereby request the following-named persons, to wit· N. P. H. Barrett, Read Benedict, John Q. Simonson, John S. Sprague, Wm. Greer, Ward McLean, Dr. Frank G. Johnson, Geo. F. Heal, Mulford D. Simonson, to inquire, and inform us at our next meeting what action is necessary for us to take in order to conform to the statutes of the state of New York, also to prepare or cause to be prepared such papers as may be concluded in such statutory re-requirements, also to ascertain and report at our next meeting about a suitable place of worship, if any can be had, and on what terms and conditions; and what arrangements can be made for preaching until the next meeting of the Newark conference; also to consult with our presiding elder on the situation generally; also to ascertain and report as above, in so far as they may be able, what other persons. male or female, would like to join our society; and whether we have legal title to any portion of the property of Trinity M. E. Church, of Factoryville (Port Richmond). Most of us are members of the said church. We hereby request the above-named persons to prepare and report at our next meeting the draft of a letter to our pastor, the Rev. Abraham Owen, asking him for our several letters, and informing him in the best possible spirit and the kindest possible terms our reasons for the course which we hereby decide upon. And we do hereby mutually exhort each other to most earnest prayer and faithful, so that God may bless our enterprise and help us to be followers of him "who, when he was reviled, reviled not again." We will pray especially that we may have grace to refrain from all unkind and uncharitable remarks to or about our brethren of Trinity Church, and as far as possible from all reference, the very object of this movement being to secure, not less than for ourselves, fraternal union and harmony, which otherwise seems to have been unattainable, and without which God's cause can not be honored. If such fraternal union and harmony as we hope and pray may result to all concerned from this act of separation, we hope for a greater degree of prosperity to each church and society than could otherwise be realized by the one."

This paper was unanimously approved. At the next meeting, held January 14th, 1867, Mr. McLean reported that the presiding elder approved of their course; Mr. Benedict reported that the committee had secured the use of the North Baptist Church for one service on Sunday and one service during the week.

At a meeting of the society held January 22nd, Ward McLean, Read Benedict and John Q. Simonson were appointed a committee to wait upon the presiding elder and the Rev. George Hughes, of Newark, (the latter whom it was proposed to call as pastor) and notify them that certain members of Trinity had drawn their certificates and were ready to be formally organized as a church.

A committee on real estate, consisting of John Q. Simonson, Wm. Bamber, Ward Mc Lean, Read Benedict, Philip H. Rustin, N. P. H. Barrett and Wm. Greer, was then appointed; also a finance committee, consisting of F. G. Johnson, Frank W. Barrett, Geo. F. Heal, Mrs. Read Benedict and Mrs. Ward McLean.

J. S. Sprague was appointed temporary superintendent, John Q. Simonson assistant superintendent, M. D. Simonson secretary, and Frank N. Barrett treasurer. William Greer, J. Q. Simonson and N. P. H. Barrett were appointed class-leaders, and Read Benedict, Ward McLean, John Q. Simonson, John S. Sprague and George F. Heal were appointed stewards.

The presiding elder was present at the next meeting held at the North Baptist Church January 23rd, and was called to the chair. The article drawn up at the meeting held at Read Benedict's was presented to him by Ward McLean on behalf of the above-named persons, with the request that they be made a separate church. This was granted and the following are the names of those who seceded from Trinity:

John Q. Simonson.

Sarah A. Simonson.

Mulford D. Simonson.

Sarah E. Simonson.

Elizabeth S. Simonson.

N. P. H. Barrett.

Annie M. Barrett.

Frank M. Barrett.

Horace F. Barrett.

Mary Coffee.

Henrietta Mc Lean.

Wm. Greer.

Catherine A. Greer.

Geo. F. Heal.

Maria Walltears.

Elizabeth Walltears.

Emily L. Wilson.

Eliza J. Seawood.

Mary Brooks.

Wm. Bamber.

John Sprague.
Mary Agnes Sprague.
Agnes E. Sgrague.
Martha A. Jones.
Josephine Johnson.
Elias Baldwin.
Thomas Taylor.
Matthew S. Taylor.
Elizabeth G. Alston.
Armenia Alston.
Sedate M. Turner.
Robt. I. Brown.

Frank G. Johnson.
Mary F. Williams.
Wm. H. Perry.
Elizabeth Perry.
Anna M. Perry.
Geo. W. Cunningham.
Susan N. Cunningham.
Alice Booth.
Isaac W. Fullager.
Read Benedict.
Mary E. Benedict.
Ward Mc Lean.

Elizabeth A. Johnson.

At the first service held Jan. 27th, 1867, the Rev. H. Hurlburt, of Orange, N. J., officiated in the absence of the Rev. George Hughes. Mr. Hughes began the first pastorate of the new church the following Sunday. The first meeting for the election of trustees was held on Monday, Feb. 18th, at the North Baptist Church, and resulted as follows: Read Benedict, Ward McLean, John Q. Simonson, Wm. Greer, N. P. H. Barrett, John S. Sprague, Wm. Bamber, Dr. Frank G. Johnson and Geo. F. Heal, and the name of Grace Methodist Episcopal Church of Port Richmond was unamiously adopted. The trustees organized by electing the following officers: Dr. F. G. Johnson, president; Read Benedict, treasurer; and Ward Mc Lean secretary. Dr. Johnson and Read Benedict were appointed a committee to purchase the lot on Heberton avenue, now occupied by the church and parsonage, and on March 17th the Tabernacle was ready for use. This was only a temporary building to accommodate the congregation until a chapel could be built.

The following account of the laying of the corner-stone was published by the *Christian Advocate*:

"The corner-stone of the Grace Methodist Episcopal Church of Port Richmond was laid with an appropriate program on Thursday last. The frowning weather doubtless prevented the attendance of many, while not a few were driven from the grounds by the rain, which commenced before the conclusion of the exercises. Nevertheless the affair was a success, and the good brethren of Grace Church have reason to be gratified by the result.

" The pastor, the Rev. A. H. Mead, was assisted by the Rev. L. R. Dunn, of Jersey City, the Rev. M. E. Ellison, of Hoboken, the Rev. N. Vansant, presiding elder of Paterson district, the Rev. J. F. Richmond, of New York, the Revs. I. H. Smith, A. H. Bellows, J. I. Morrow and J. S. Chadwick.

" The statement of the condition and prospect of the enterprise, made by the pastor, prompted the hearty congratulations of the brethren of the ministry who were present.

" The society have ample grounds for a chapel, church and parsonage, together with the 'Tabernacle' in which they now worship. The chapel walls, as they now stand, and considerable building material, are all paid for.

" The chapel is to be an economical and tasteful structure 32x65 ft., which the society hope to finish before the coming winter.

" The pastor was followed by Mr. Dunn, who delivered an eloquent address. Mr. Ellison made an appeal which was characterized by unusual spirit, tact and ingenuity, and which was responded to with commendable liberality. Among the interesting articles and documents that were deposited in the corner-stone were copies of the Bible, the discipline, and some of the principal secular papers, a copy of the *Christian Advocate*, the *Methodist*, also of the *Richmond County Gazette*.

" The occasion was enlivened with some choice selections of music, which were well rendered by the choir and an anthem was sung by the congregation which had been written especially for the occasion by Dr. Johnson, one of the trustees of the church."

The church was dedicated on Sunday Dec. 29th, 1867, with preaching at 10:30 a. m. by the Rev. L. R. Dunn, also at 3:30, and at 7 p. m. by the Rev. Alexander Mead.

The services were continued on the following Sunday, when the pulpit was occupied by the Rev. Dr. Porter of the Book Room, New York, both morning and evening.

The chapel was much admired, both its architecture and furnishings. The financial results of the dedicatory services were very encouraging. The pastor announced that if $3,000 were raised the floating indebtedness would be canceled. To reach this result the Sunday-school offered to raise $500, and two individuals would each pledge $500 provided the congregation would make up the balance—$1,500. This was accomplished on dedication day—the succeeding Sunday.

The winter following was attended by a revival, in which 24 confessed conversion, most of whom afterwa d joined the church. Mr. Mead remained its pastor until the September of 1868, when he was succeeded by the Rev. P. D. Day, who preached his first sermon on September 20th.

In August 1872, the church was frescoed and painted at a cost of about $500.

In April 1873, the envelope system of subscriptions was adopted. At the same time classes were organized and neighborhood prayer-meetings established, for which five leaders were appointed.

On May 25th, 1873, the Sunday-school was reorganized, and a disciplinary constitution and new by-laws were adopted. This is still known as "reorganization day." At the same time Phillip Waters was elected superintendent, and the "Grace M. E. S. S." monogram stamp was first introduced, and June 8th following, 20 new Sunday-school banners were presented to the classes.

On July 20th, 1873, the Rev. Dr. Dashiell officiated and subscriptions were obtained to cover the expense of furnishing the parsonage. *Fruits of Grace*, a journal published in the interest of the Sunday-school and church, was first issued in September, 1873. In the same month, the "Ladies' and Pastor's Christian Union" was organized and the constitution adopted.

The following spring, the pastor, the Rev. J. J. Reed, Jr., was removed by an Episcopal appointment and was succeeded by the Rev W. T. Gill. During the first year of Mr. Gill's pastorate, notwithstanding the hard times, $1,100 were paid on the floating debt beside all the current expenses.

During the pastorate of the Rev. R. S. Arndt the new parsonage was built.

In July 1895, a fire occurred in the church which made it necessary to find some other suitable place in which to hold services, and the permission of the trustees of the public school was obtained, and it was then decided, instead of repairing the damage done by the fire, to tear down the old building and to erect a new church on the same site.

The corner-stone of the new Grace Church was laid December 11th, 1895, by the Rev. Dr. C. S. Ryman. Mulford D. Simonson, the treasurer, gave the following financial report: Subscriptions received, $6,562; profits on the fair recently held in Griffith Hall, $1,000, making a total of $7,562. The estimated cost of the church and organ was $25,000. The Rev. J. G. Johnston, pastor of the church, then called for further subscriptions, and an additional $1,500 was raised, making a total of $9,062 toward the new building when the foundation stone was laid.

The *Christian Advocate* gives the following account of the dedication services and the description of the new church:

"The new building of this society—the Rev. J. G. Johnston, pastor—was opened for service Sunday, Feb. 14th. The Rev. H. A. Buttz, D. D., president of Drew Seminary, preached the opening sermon. The Rev. Dr. G. W. Smith, presiding elder of Elizabeth district, preached in the afternoon, and the Rev. John Krantz preached in the evening and conducted the financial effort all day. Large audiences made ready response to his able appeals, and over $4,000 were secured. A young people's rally was arranged for Monday evening, and addresses were made by Mr. A. M. Harris and two former pastors, the Revs. C. E. Little and Jesse S. Gilbert. Tuesday evening, the pastors of six denominations extended their fraternal greetings, and on Wednesday evening the Rev. J. R. Bryan, D. D., and the Rev. Francis A. Mason spoke the congratulations of their people and represented the Methodism of Staten Island. Thursday evening an organ recital and concert was given under the able direction of Mrs. Winfield S. McCowan, wife of the pastor of St. Paul's Church, to a large and delighted audience. Friday evening the Revs. C. E. Dutcher and W. B. Wigg were present and addressed the people in happy vein, and letters were received from the Rev. John Coyle, D. D., of California ; the Rev. A. J. Palmer, D. D., and the Rev. John J. Reed, D. D., former pastors. Sunday morning, Feb. 21st, Bishop Hurst preached the sermon and dedicated the church. The Rev. Joseph A. Owen brought this series of services to a close with a sermon in the evening.

" The new building is of Gothic style and is sixty feet front by seventy-five feet deep, built of dark brick and trimmed with terra cotta. The stone steps lead up the terrace and, diverging, ascend to the porches in the towers on the two corners of the front. One tower ends in a castellated turret, the other leads up to a graceful steeple 100 feet above. Inside, the floor inclines with a gentle grade to the pulpit, and is seated with comfortable circular pews made of yellow birch, and will accommodate about 500. The organ loft is back of the pulpit, containing seats for the choir and a grand organ of fine tone, and decorated with exquisite taste in harmony with the other furnishings, which are bright and cheerful. An improved steam heater works admirably in keeping the church most comfortable in the severest weather;

stained glass windows of pleasing tints afford
abundant light; while an electric apparatus of
latest scientific order illuminates most brilliantly
at night. The Sunday-school, with its fine primary
department, has beautiful accommodations, as
have also the young people's society, the Ladies'
Aid Society and the other organizations of the
church. The expenses are all provided for, with
the exception of about $2,000. The church is a
great addition to the neighborhood, and gives a
new and firmer hold for Methodism in this locality."

LIST OF PASTORS.

1867-8—A. H. Mead, supernumerary, residence in
Meriden, Conn.

1868—Peter D. Day, died at New Providence, N. J.,
Oct. 10th, 1888, aged 77 years: 56 years in
ministry.

1869-71—John Coyle, moved from conference, residence in California.

1872—A. J. Palmer, corresponding secretary of the
Missionary Society, New York.

1873—J. J. Reed, stationed at Yonkers, N. Y.

1874-6—W. I. Gill.

1877—Thompson H. Landon, principal Bordentown,
N. J., Military Institute; entered ministry in
1857.

1878—Joseph A. Owens, stationed at Elizabeth, N. J.;
entered ministry in 1874.

1879-81—Jesse S. Gilbert, stationed at Spring Valley, N. Y.; entered ministry in 1867.

1882-3—Edward C. Dutcher, stationed in Jersey
City, N. J.; entered ministry in 1878.

1884-6—Ralph S. Arndt, died in Newark, N. J., Aug.
17th, 1892, aged 66 years; 43 years in ministry.

1887-91—Charles E. Little, stationed in Jersey City, N. J.; entered ministry in 1860.

1892 6—J. G. Johnston, stationed at Bloomfield, N. J.; entered ministry in 1877.

1897—A. C. McCrea, present pastor; entered ministry in 1895.

LADIES' AID SOCIETY:

The Ladies' Aid Society was organized June 21st, 1892, and has 42 members. The first officers chosen were as follows:

Mrs. Mulford D. Simonson, president; Mrs. George Granger, vice-president; Mrs. Henry L. Simonson, secretary; Mrs. Xiques, treasurer.

The officers elected at the last election are:

Mrs. W. J. Bailey, president; Mrs. J. W. Wood, vice-president; Mrs. F. M. Simonson, secretary; Mrs. Henry L. Simonson, treasurer.

KING'S DAUGHTERS:

The circle of King's Daughters was organized Jan. 15th, 1894, with officers as follows:

Miss Gertrude Xiques, president; Miss Mamie Benedict, vice-president; Miss Decker, secretary; Miss Summers, treasurer.

The officers in charge at the present time:

Mrs. Harry E. Heal, president; Mrs. A. C. McCrea, vice-president; Mrs. W. H. Mitchill, secretary; Mrs. Nelson Hersh, treasurer.

PRESENT MEMBERSHIP.

Mr. and Mrs. Japhet Alston.
     "   Henry Beatty.
     "   Joseph Bailey.
     "   William H. Bailey.
     "   Wm. J. Bailey.
     "   John J. Becker.

Mr. and Mrs. Read Benedict.
  "   Sanford S. Blair.
  "   Robert P. Brown.
  "   C. M. Braisted.
  "   Gilbert Benedict.
  "   W. H. Depuy.
  "   H. W. Depuy.
  "   George Decker.
  "   John H. Decker.
  "   C. T. Elms.
  "   John A. Franklin.
  "   G. O. Granger.
  "   S. M. Giles.
  "   A. J. F. Goessling.
  "   Simon J. Houghwout.
  "   O. H. Hoag.
  "   Jesse Houghwout.
  "   W. J. McMillan.
  "   Harry E. Manee.
  "   A. E. Mosher.
  "   J. E. Marchant.
  "   G. S. Mawhinney.
  "   E. Parker.
  "   Peter Peters.
  "   W. S. Piercey.
  "   H. J. Sharrett.
  "   Thomas J. Simonson.
  "   Mulford D. Simonson.
  "   Henry L. Simonson.
  "   William Stewart.
  "   Fred M. Simonson.
  "   Harry A. Simonson.
  "   I. A. Silvie.
  "   Frank Xiques.

Mr. and Mrs E. Westburgh.
  " Albert Vroom.
  " J. W. Wortz.
  " Andrew Hagamann.
  " W. L. Hawkins.
  " G. H. Janeman.
  " Griffith Jennings.
  " J. Lisk.
  " Theodore Lewis.
  " J. H. Anderson.
  " M. Christensen.
  " H. J. Wilsher.
  " James Walker.
Dr. and Mrs. E. D. Coonley.
  " J. Walter Wood.
Mrs. E. D. Velzer.
  " S. J. Lloyd.
  " Wm. M. Schneider.
  " S. C. Mawhinney.
  " Thomas McBurney.
  " Charles B. Pollock.
  " Harry E. Heal.
  " E. J. Muddell.
  " W. H. Mitchell.
  " E. de Lille.
  " M. E. Wygant.
  " James V. Burkman.
  " A. Mott.
  " L. H. Achilles.
  " Margaret Decker.
  " Marjorie Davis.
  " Frances Bush.
  " Maria Belknap.
  " Mary Brown.

Mrs. Mary Vroom.
  " Mary Perry.
  " Mary J. Kinney.
  " Elizabeth J. Leonard.
  " Ann Bailey.
  " Mary E. Brown.
  " Mary G. Rand.
  " Mary C. Renton.
  " Abby Simonson.
  " Tillie Olmstead.
  " Sarah F. Heal.
  " Ellen Davis.
  " Anna M. Doyle.
  " Lina Elder.
  " Martha B. Calvert.
  " Eliza J. Davis.
Miss Dency E. Becker.
  " Mary E. Coonley.
  " Laura Bailey.
  " Mary E. Deye,
  " Eva Giles.
  " Susie Giles.
  " Julia Giles.
  " Addie Goessling.
  " Ella Heal.
  " Reta McMillan.
  " Muriel McMillan.
  " Ada M. Marchant.
  " C. E. Price.
  " S. Price.
  " Lorena Price.
  " Lillian Stewart.
  " Ella Johnson.
  " Cammilla Lister.

Miss S. W. Vroom.
    "   Gertrude Wilsher.
    "   Mabel Slater.
    "   Annie Wilsher.
    "   Agnes E. Wood.
    "   Leonora Wortz.
    "   Mary E. Mawhinney
    "   Julia Sharrott.
Mr. A. I. Silvie.
    "   Read B. Simonson.
    "   Robert Xiques.
    "   Elwood Wood.
    "   William Houghwout.
    "   Fred. S. Heal.
    "   James King.
    "   Fred L. Kinney.
    "   Washington A. Reardon.
    "   Harmon Speer.
    "   Frank R. Simonson.
    "   J. H. Silvie.
    "   Frank Marchant.
    "   R. B. Peters.
    "   William Houghwout.
    "   Everett Lancey.
    "   W. H. D. Mullin.
    "   John Decker.
    "   Horatio Braisted.
    "   DeWitt C. Crocheron.
    "   William H. Blair.
    "   Arthur F. Brassington.
    "   William H. DeHart.
    "   Alvin Depuy.
    "   Frank Becker.
    "   Henry Becker.

Mr. Sandford J. Becker.
  " Emil Bottger.
  " Wm. A. Anderson.
  " William A. Anderson, Jr.
  " Charles A. Anderson.
  " Charles P. Benedict.
  " Coleman Benedict.
  " Frederick Coonley.
  " Theo. H. Spratt.
Capt. Clarence E. Underhill.

www.ingramcontent.com/pod-product-compliance
Lightning Source LLC
Chambersburg PA
CBHW021215270326
41929CB00010B/1139